WOMEN AND THE MAKING OF THE WORKING CLASS:
LYON 1830~1870

Laura S. Strumingher

EDEN PRESS

Monographs in
Women's Studies

Series Editor:
Sherri Clarkson

WOMEN AND THE MAKING OF THE WORKING CLASS:
LYON 1830~1870

Laura S. Strumingher

© **Eden Press Women's Publications, Inc. 1979**

Published by:
Eden Press Women's Publications, Inc.
Box 51, St. Alban's, Vermont 05478 U.S.A.
and
Eden Press Women's Publications,
1538 Sherbrooke St. West, #201, Montreal, Quebec, Canada H3G 1L5

ISBN 0-88831-027-7
Library of Congress Catalog Card Number 78-74841

Dépôt légal - première trimestre 1979
Bibliothèque nationale du Québec

Typeset in Century Textbook, 10 point on 12, by
Vicky Bach, Hamilton

Printed in Brattleboro, Vermont, U.S.A.

For Serge, Eric, and Neil

CONTENTS

PREFACE

In 1848 Karl Marx stated: "Workers of the world unite, you have nothing to lose but your chains!" Since that time many historians have pondered the question, why did the workers fail to unite in England or France throughout the remainder of the nineteenth century? As a young historian, I too have pondered this question. My study of working men and women in Lyon, France's second city of the nineteenth century, has given me an answer to this intriguing enigma. It is my hypothesis that the men and women workers acquired different perspectives on their positions as workers; in fact, the gap between them was more basic and more influential than the frequently cited differences between skilled and non-skilled workers, or city and rural workers. My theory is that the division between men and women workers slowed the development of the working class, by confusing proletarian consciousness with debates on the appropriate sphere for women workers.

Ten years ago as a beginning graduate student at the University of Rochester, I was introduced to E.P. Thompson's important, *The Making of the English Working Class*. Thompson focused the study of class by his astute emphasis on process:

> *class happens when some men, as a result of common experiences (inherited or shared), feel and articulate the identity of their interests as between themselves, and as against other men whose interests are different from (and usually opposed to) theirs.* [1]

But working men and women shared some experiences and at the same time perceived each other as very different. Despite the similarity of their working conditions, men denied women membership in their

i

clubs and argued against women's rights to equal pay and even their right to work. It was this paradox which slowed the formation of the working class.

In 1971 Sanford Elwitt gave me the opportunity to research this problem by encouraging me to do my dissertation on the women silk workers of Lyon. The large and articulate worker population of the city provided an excellent opportunity to study both the reality of workers' lives and the myths they were encouraged to believe in by educators, both lay and clerical. I investigated how women workers reacted both to the material conditions and to the ideology of modernization, and the crucial role women played in the making of the working class.

The nineteenth century in Lyon was a time of technological innovation, expansion of credit, urbanization, political upheavals, as well as changes remains in the archives. Archivists at the National Archives in ethic. A wealth of both impressionistic--letters, diaries, newspaper accounts, police reports, medical journals, school books--and quantitative--marriage registers, arrest records, censuses--evidence of these changes remains in the Archives. Archivists at the National Archives in Paris helped me commence my search. Later on, Lyon's Municipal Archives and Municipal Library were rich in sources and pleasant to work in.

Lyon is very fortunate to have a comradely group of scholars who were all very helpful to me. Special mention must be given to Professor Yves Lequin of the Université de Lyon II whose encouragement of my project was constant and very much appreciated. George Sheridan was a graduate student working on his dissertation when I first arrived in Lyon; his help in finding "lost" volumes was invaluable. Natalie Davis and Robert Bezucha both read parts of my manuscript at an early stage and provided useful criticism and suggestions.

Several other colleagues and friends have read all or parts of the manuscript and I wish to thank them for their help: Sanford Elwitt, John Merriman, Peter Stearns, Edward Shorter, Louise Tilly, Joan Scott, Roger Daniels, William T. Hagan, Robert P. Neuman, Milton Cantor, and Michelle Perrot. They have greatly contributed to the improvement of the manuscript; any shortcomings that remain are my own.

A university of Rochester Graduate Fellowship made possible my first extended stay in Paris in 1971, and in 1974 and 1975 SUNY Faculty Research Grants enabled me to spend summers in Lyon to complete the research. I also wish to thank several journals who have been kind enough to allow me to include in the manuscript parts of articles they have already published: *Cahiers d'Histoire, Societas, Journal of Family History* and *Journal of Social History.*

A special note of thanks to Arlene O'Leary, my high school history teacher, who first introduced me to the joys of intellectual endeavor, and to Mary Notaro whose typing and retyping made this project a reality.

Motto: "On oublie un peu trop le malheureux sort des femmes de la classe ouvrière. . . ."

Tribune Lyonnaise
September 1848

Chapter I

THE DEMISE OF THE FAMILY WORKSHOP

At the beginning of the nineteenth century, the Rhône valley was unable to produce enough food to satisfy the needs of its 300,000 inhabitants. The grain harvest provided for only one-third of the year and the peasants ate mainly potatoes. During the next decades, the problem worsened as the population of the region nearly doubled, reaching 575,000 by 1851.[1] About 137,000 of this increase was composed of native peasants, creating a corresponding increase in demand on the local food supply. More and more of them had to find another source of income to pay for food which had to be brought from the rest of France. The other half of the increase in the population of the area from 1800 to 1851 was due to immigration.

Situated in the center of this valley on a plain about two miles long, between the banks of the Rhône and the Saône, is Lyon, the capital of the French silk industry. The Restoration brought peace and prosperity to Lyon and the rustle of activity attracted many of the neighboring peasants and the immigrants from other regions of France, and from Italy and Switzerland. They massed especially in the suburb of the Croix-Rousse which hovered over the city on a steep mountain slope. There, flats with ceilings tall enough to accommodate the new Jacquard silk looms were built.[2] The population of the Croix-Rousse doubled from 6,000 in 1800 to 12,000 in 1829; in 1825 and 1840 inundations of the Saône forced silk workers to flee from the neighboring villages of Vaise and Brotteaux; many of them went to the Croix-Rousse where the population reached 19,000 in 1841. Towards the end of the decade, 9,000 more men and women crowded to the place, bringing the total

1

population to 28,000.[3] This caprice of nature, the jutting mountain on which the workers dwelled, strikingly underlined the social divisions of the city.

The physical separation represented by the Croix-Rousse also reflected the growing economic and social gap between the successful silk merchants and the growing numbers of silk workers during our period. The merchants remembered the rebellions of 1831 and 1834 and feared another uprising which might cut their revenues for several months and put them out of business as the silk industry had entered a period of massive concentration. The male workers, called *canuts,* were formerly artisan weavers who worked at home. They resented the merchants who lowered them to the status of workshop proletarians, stripping them of their pride and independence. The women workers, the *canutes,* were formerly peasant women who used to engage in part-time reeling, or weavers' wives who used to assist their husbands at home. They resented the merchants for moving their work away from home while continuing to pay them less than subsistence wages. This left the young women with no other choice but marry early or move in with a male worker in order to survive.

Spurred on by several technical developments affecting all stages of the silk industry, from raw materials to finished fabric, the 1840's were a period of marked transition for the silk entrepreneurs and their employees. New techniques in the production of silk cocoons increased six-fold the quantity of raw silk produced in France from 1815 to 1848.[4] Simultaneously, improvements in the machinery used for pulling and reeling silk fiber, plus the application of steam to the process, also increased the quantity and the quality of silk thread,[5] while the spreading use of the Jacquard loom enabled the weavers to produce a greater quantity of intricately patterned silk fabric.[6]

The number of looms in Lyon and its surrounding villages increased rapidly under the July Monarchy. To the 27,000 looms operating at the end of the Restoration, 13,000 new looms were added by 1833.[7] Most of them were of the improved Jacquard type which removed the necessity for a draw-boy and produced 25% more cloth per day. From 1830, the number of looms in the city proper remained stationary at about 30,000 while their number in the surrounding countryside--in the

Departments of the Loire, Saône-et-Loire, Ain, Isère, and Drôme--grew from 5,263 in 1833 to 30,500 in 1840.[8] This phenomenon was due to a conscious effort on the part of employers to disperse workers to the countryside in order to prevent urban riots. Thus, by the end of our period there were about 65,000 looms in the Lyon area of which only half were in the city and its suburbs. The Jacquard looms, used primarily for weaving luxury silks, and fitting in the Croix-Rousse buildings, had replaced many of the old looms in the city and suburbs while the old looms moved out to the countryside and were used for making plain, unpatterned silks.[9]

In the 1830's and the early 1840's economic expansion was not unique to Lyon. It was a period of prosperity for all of France. The national wealth grew more than twice as fast as the population during the July Monarchy.[10] All of this excess wealth was absorbed by a limited number of the bourgeoisie who spent it conspicuously on fancy dress and furnishings, but who, more significantly, also invested it. Many placed large sums in the Bank of France which opened up branch offices in the provinces, spreading the availability of credit and the mobility of capital.[11] Simultaneously the Bourse (Stock Exchange) in Paris expanded due to increasing interest in investments from offering 44 stocks in 1836 to 204 in 1844. Huge investments in industrial developments were made in the same period.[12]

As we saw, in the Lyon area these investments resulted in doubling the number of looms for silk weaving. Only now that Lyon was able to produce ever-increasing quantities of silk, she had to find a way to increase the demand for it. Exports to the U.S. and England, and smaller exports to Germany, Belgium, Spain, Russia, Italy, Mexico, Brazil and Turkey accounted for as much as 80% of Lyonese silk production during the period 1833-43.[13] But, in 1837 and in 1842, when the American and English markets were sharply contracted by depressions, Lyonese merchants recognized the necessity to develop the domestic market for silk. By November 1844, 50% of the silk produced in Lyon was aimed at internal consumption;[14] but the increase occurred mainly in the volume of lower grade silk and in the output of mixed fabrics whose price was within reach of city petty bourgeoisie.

Nevertheless, the average annual value of silk imports from Lyon climbed steadily from the end of the Napoleonic period to the Revolution of 1848 and throughout our period, regardless of the frequent fluctuations in demand, the big profits remained in luxury silks for export.[15] Eighty million francs of Lyonese silk were exported annually between 1815 and 1822. The sum increased to 112 million during the decade 1825-35 and reached 139 million francs per year the following decade.[16] In 1846, a smaller increase in the average annual export to only 146 million, reflected the temporary decline in the silk industry. By 1847, prosperity was returning to the Lyonese entrepreneurs, who did 165 million francs of export business.[17]

The drive, in the thirties and forties, to create a domestic market for plain silk and mixed cloths, so as to reduce dependence on foreign markets, succeeded only because new techniques for weaving waste silk copied from the cotton industry, were introduced.[18] The fragments of threads and strands from inferior cocoons which had previously been discarded were now used in simple silks and silk combined with wool, cotton, and linen. These fabrics, produced for the domestic market, provided jobs for less skilled workers, increasing mainly the number of *canutes.*

In 1845, when the silk industry was juggling to balance the unreliable export silks with the more reliable but less profitable domestic silks by investing large sums in new machinery, to produce increased amounts of both qualities, crisis struck. Throughout France 1845-46 was a period of crop failures and bad harvests. This created an urgent need to buy agricultural products abroad. As crop failures were simultaneously plaguing the whole of western Europe,[19] the dilemma was so much the worse.

Bad harvests were at the root of the economic troubles in France, but severely restricted liquidity, resulting from large investments in banking and industry in the 1830's and speculation in railroads and public works in which Lyonese silk merchants participated heavily in the 1840's, sharply aggravated the crisis.[20] Between 1840 and 1847, 630 million francs were invested in French railroads, while the Ministry of Public Works issued bonds for one billion francs and the Ministry of

War collected 260 million francs, including 140 million for the fortification of Paris. The total seven-year investment was 1.9 billion francs. [21]

The dramatic fall in the reserves of the Bank of France reflected the gravity of the crisis. On January 1, 1846, the Bank had 225 million francs in reserves. One year later, the reserves had dropped to 80 million, and by mid-January 1847, the reserves had plunged to 59 million francs. The Bank adopted four measures to strengthen its reserves: it coined 5 million francs in silver; it secured 5 million francs from provincial branches; it borrowed 25 million francs from the Barings of England; and it raised the discount rate from 4 to 5 %. It took all of 1847 for these measures to revitalize the economy. So, ironically, the February Revolution of 1848 broke out as the crisis was waning. [22]

For the Lyonese silk entrepreneurs the aggregate influence of technological innovation, of the boom period 1827-33, [23] followed by a decade of more moderate growth, and culminating with the crisis of 1845-47, just reviewed, resulted in a tremendous concentration of property. The generally adverse financial conditions of 1845 caught in their grips the extremely competitive silk industry. And as always with such industries their expansion was based on debt financing which rendered individual entrepreneurs vulnerable to tight money conditions. That explains why so many went out of business due to indebtedness motivated by expansion and modernization and their businesses fell into the hands of the financially strong amongst their competitors, some of whom had been lenders of money against equipment as collateral.

The new machines required significant capital investment--one Jacquard loom cost between 400 and 4,000 francs [24] --which only a minority of silk merchants could afford, the result was that the number of silk enterprises decreased sharply during our period. This was a clear reversal of trend from the steady proliferation of silk merchants and their businesses which had multiplied seven times during the period 1811-1831, from 50 merchants to 750. [25] The following twenty-year period witnessed this dramatic consolidation of silk enterprises. For example, in 1843 only, 86 silk business failures were reported in Lyon, [26] and in the ten-month period from April 1844 to January 1845,

42 more failures were recorded, [27] so that by 1850 only 300 enterprises remained, owned by 450 businessmen.

Most significantly, the amount of business done by the top 50 of these entrepreneurs equalled that of all the others combined. As Claude Aboucaya has demonstrated, a minority of businessmen accumulated considerable fortunes, while the majority lost ground. [28] Successful merchants assumed a more active role in the manufacturing process.

The technological improvements, contraction in the demand for luxury silk, and the crisis of 1845-47, described above, not only consolidated the wealth in the hands of a few silk entrepreneurs, it also meant falling wages and recurrent unemployment for the silk workers. For example, velvet weavers, who earned seven francs per day in 1842 were only able to earn three francs per day in 1844. [29] Prices for velvet weaving remained even in 1845, but dropped another 20% in 1846. [30] The price paid for weaving figured shawls declined similarly in the 1840's from eight francs per shawl to 2 fr 50 per shawl. Even the most skillful and hardworking weaver could not make more than one and a half shawls per day, earning 3 fr 75. Weavers of plain silk, who were usually paid between one and two francs per day also took a 5-10% wage cut in 1846. [31] When the weavers suffered wage decreases, they passed on the decrease to their assistants: the reelers, winders, warpers. Frequently they postponed paying their assistants for long periods, and simply seized their work to pay off pressing bills. [32]

In the mid-forties slackening of demand resulted in great numbers of idle looms and a narrowing of the spectrum of products, though, simultaneously looms which were employed in weaving novelty items to satisfy the whims of fashionable women in the United States and England had become numerous by 1846. This was due to the temptation to create ever more designs to beat the competitors. [33] But although these fads knew temporary success in the beginning of 1846, 33% of the looms making novelty silks were idle from November 1846 to March 1847. [34]

The demand for shawls also decreased in late 1846 and more than 1,000 looms which were usually employed in making shawls remained idle

6

throughout the winter; since every two looms provided employment for five people, 2500 shawl makers were without jobs. They joined the unemployed velvet makers, satin makers, mixed textile makers, and patterned silk makers. In the winter of 1846-47 these unemployed amounted to 60% of the silk labor force of 200,000. [35]

Falling wages and widespread unemployment hastened the demise of the family workshop where a master craftsman (*chef d'atelier*), aided by his wife and children, employed a few journeymen and apprentices. Typically, the master owned four to six looms and worked on consignment for a merchant. These family workshops had been the production center for Lyonese silks for centuries. Under the Restoration they proliferated because masters were easily able to open their own workshops on the advances they received from merchants. The money was quickly repaid by the increasing value of the weaver's labor. [36] But this situation did not last long because production soon exceeded demand, as we pointed out above, and by the mid-forties masters were no longer able to hire journeymen or apprentices, because the cost of feeding them was greater than the money they could earn. Journeymen could no longer look forward to becoming master craftsmen, nor to setting up their own workshops because they could not buy the looms nor the flats, as their weaving skills were no longer sufficient collateral. [37]

The family workshops could not compete with the larger workshops and factories opened by the silk entrepreneurs in the late '30's and early '40's. The improved machinery bought by silk manufacturers, which increased the quantity and quality of production, was beyond the reach of the master craftsman. [38] Growth in the supply of labor and contraction in the demand for silk brought wages down and during the crisis of the mid-forties forced many masters to give up their looms and their shops and become itinerant weavers again. [39] The word *compagnon* which traditionally meant a journeyman on his way to becoming a master, was by 1845 used to denote all male weavers who owned no looms. Simultaneously, the word *compagnonne* was created to designate a new group of weavers--the women. Women weavers came to the fore when they displaced their husbands at the now low-paying weaving jobs while the latter sought more lucrative work, often as coal miners, and after 1850 in the expanding metallurgical industry. [40]

7

The displacement of men weavers by women, a result of falling wages and the break-up of family workshops began in the early 1840's with the increasing demand for cheap labor to weave plain silks for the domestic market. Women were hired to weave plain silk increasingly from 1840; by 1847, plain silk weaving was almost exclusively a female occupation. Concomitantly, decreased demand for figured weavers resulted in falling numbers of men employed as journeymen. Figured weaving continued to be primarily a male province until the introduction of steam-powered looms in the sixties.

Itinerant weavers of both sexes differed from the master artisan in several important ways, not the least of which was the fact that they were "specialized" as weavers and knew little about the preliminary aspects of setting up the loom which became several distinct jobs performed in separate workshops. The master craftsman of previous generations knew a great deal about this preparatory work, having participated in it as a youth and directed his apprentices or family in it as a master. With the coming of the itinerant weavers we see the deterioration of the knowledgeable craftsman who became a specialized worker dependent on an increasingly complicated machine.

With the collapse of the family workshops, and the introduction of bigger machines silk entrepreneurs needed a new location for their weavers and other *canutes* to work. Instead of investing money in new factory buildings, the Lyonese businessmen developed a very success-ful alternative solution--they financed workshops within the numerous convents surrounding Lyons. Reeling, winding, warping, and weaving workshops were set up in La Sainte-Famille, La Providence, Le Sacré-Coeur, La Solitude, and others. Loans to purchase the machinery were financed by the silk merchants, while the nuns directed the workshops. The nuns paid off their debts by selling their silk fabric back to the merchants. They always had customers because they charged less than the individual master weavers. [41]

The convent workshops were uniquely suited for employing large numbers of women. The zealous nuns made remarkable forewomen, directing their *canutes* to work faster and more diligently. The convent was also able to provide cheap food and lodgings for the women workers. This was doubly beneficial since it allowed the nuns to pay their workers only a small fraction of the daily wage received by women who had to pay for their own food and lodgings, and second, it prevented the women from having any contact with the rebellious workers in the city. [42]

The master weavers who continued to lose their shops, their looms and even their professions during the forties singled out the convent-workshop, supported by the silk tycoons, as their special enemy. [43] They complained that establishments in which laborers worked and lived together were unfair competition to the individual weaver. [44] Some demanded the right for workers to organize into large cooperative workshops of their own, which were illegal, to be able to compete with the low prices of the convents. Others urged that a tax be imposed on convents which manufactured and that the proceeds of the tax be used to help workers.

The consensus of worker opinion was that the convents, ostensibly religious communities which established workshops to provide employment and thus help the poor, actually hurt them by exploiting young women of worker families and competing unfairly with the master weavers. [45] But the master weavers never demanded that the convent-workshop pay higher wages to the women employed there. This would have forced the nuns to raise the price of their silk and possibly made the work of the family workshops competitive. Though they clearly recognized that the young women working in the convents were being exploited, they did not view them as fellow workers whose demands for higher wages should be supported. Instead they persistently, though unsuccessfully, demanded higher prices for their own work from the merchants.

In 1844 the master weavers brought their problems to the attention of the silk merchants by circulating a petition which reiterated their demands for a liveable income first proclaimed in 1831 and 1834-- *"Vivre en Travaillant."* They insisted on an increase in the price paid for their work. Several merchants agreed that their request was just and promised to give their weavers a raise if all the merchants would agree to do the same. [46] It is not surprising that an agreement was never reached. Why should the merchants raise the minimum wage for their master weavers when they could hire more women at one franc per day? The family workshop which was already under attack in the early forties because of falling wages and periodic unemployment for the master craftsmen received further blows with each new woman weaver who entered the job market.

Curtet, a former master weaver from the Croix-Rousse, who had been forced to give up his family workshop and his looms at 19 rue de Mail, provided us with a detailed account of the financial instability of the family workshops in the mid-forties. (See Appendix A.) His account of a typical master weaver's balance sheet including all revenue and expenditures during the 12 months from May 1844 to May 1845, a fairly prosperous period for weavers, [47] revealed a deficit of 277 francs. The master he described owned four looms, one which he worked himself, while the other three were worked by journeymen.

The first loom in the shop was set up for five different jobs during the year. It was used to weave 143 meters of fabric for satin collars, 200 meters of plain silk for undergarments, 48 meters of cashmere for vests, and 100 meters of fabric for novelty vests. The fifth job was cancelled during production. The total annual revenue for this loom was 828 francs.

The second loom was also set up five times. It was used to weave 212 meters of silk for dresses, 75 meters of silk for neckties, 130 meters of silk for buttons, 150 meters of silk for novelty vests, and another 75 meters of silk for neckties. The revenue from the second loom was 818 francs.

The third loom was set up only four times. It was used to weave 420 meters of silk and cotton for vests, 55 meters of fabric for cashmere collars, 30 meters of fabric for cashmere vests, and 200 meters of fabric for furniture upholstry. It produced a total revenue of 933 francs.

The fourth loom was set up five times. It was used to weave 36 meters of fabric for richly decorated collars, 170 meters of cashmere for collars, 180 meters of coarse silk for vests, 50 meters of mixed fabric for vests, and 75 meters of silk for ties. The total revenue from the fourth loom was 907 francs. The total revenue from all the looms plus an advance of 53 francs to purchase silk thread was 3,547 francs.

Although, as Curtet pointed out, 1844-45 was a prosperous year for the master weavers, his balance sheet revealed long periods of unemployment for the men working each of the looms. The first loom was idle for 80 days. Allowing time to set up new patterns, the loom was left standing for two months. The second loom was idle for three months; the third for only a few days, but the fourth for 45 days.

In addition to looms which were not fully employed, the balance sheet revealed another source of economic trouble for the family workshop-- inefficient use of looms. Master weavers never knew in advance what the orders would be for the next job, they had to wait for the merchant to tell them what he wanted to be woven. Therefore, they could not plan to use each loom exclusively for one pattern, which would have saved them the cost of setting up new patterns for each job. For example, the second was set up for neckties early in the year and then had to be set up again for the same pattern when a new order was placed. The fourth loom was also employed making this fabric later in the year. Each time the warp and woof for necktie fabric was set up it cost the weaver a day's wages for each of three assistants. Usually he was obliged to feed his assistants too. The balance sheet revealed similar cases when the first and third looms were individually prepared to weave cashmere vest cloth at different times. Similar wastes were involved on the third and fourth looms which were set up to weave cashmere collars. Frequent changes of patterns not only cost the weaver extra wages for reelers, winders, and warpers, it also cost him unnecessary wear of the looms. These were not minor considerations since the total cost to the weaver of setting up the fifteen jobs described above, including 100 francs for repairing the looms, was 600 francs.

In striking contrast with the master weaver's high overhead were the relatively low production costs of the silk entrepreneur, in his own weaving workshop or in the convent shop in which he had a direct interest, who decided independently what to weave. This business-man could decide several months in advance what he thought would be in demand and then assign each loom to a particular pattern. The looms were set up once for the season, and kept producing fabric, without wasting time or money in changing the patterns. In this way the businessman enjoyed a great advantage over the weaver and his family workshop.

The master weaver was unable to compete with the entrepreneur in a second and far more significant way--wages for journeymen in a family workshop were much higher than what the convent or the businessman had to pay. The master who provided instruction and the loom traditionally paid his journeymen 50% of the revenue from the loom he worked. In the case reviewed above, 50% of the revenue of the three looms worked by the journeymen totaled 1,335 francs, so that each man received an average of 445 francs for the year. Keeping in mind that they were all unemployed for an average of 50 days and that they did not work on Sundays, the journeyman earned about 1.80 francs per day (which was about average for the forties). The manufacturer, not bound by tradition, hired increasing numbers of women weavers who worked for one franc per day.

Faced with such stiff competition the master craftsman often taught his wife to weave and employed her at one loom. His children were set to preparing the warp and woof so as to save more money. But, even by cutting their standard of living considerably--not purchasing clothing, not laundering their linens, eating less expensive food--the master still had to pay the rent and to maintain the looms. When this became impossible, the master craftsman and often his wife also joined the growing numbers of itinerant weavers for hire.

The rebellions of 1831 and 1834, admirably described by Robert Bezucha, [48] were attempts to preserve rates paid by merchants to master weavers. By 1846, when the crisis pressured the weavers with further wage reductions, the *Echo d'Industrie,* a silk workers' journal, carried a copy of a new workers' petition which, it reported, had been signed by tens of thousands of workers from all over France. [49] This petition demanded that the Chamber of Deputies in Paris conduct an inquiry into the condition of all workers. They claimed that the existence of increasingly frantic competition victimized more and more workers every day. It resulted in the exaggeratedly low price for hand work and the overall lowering of wages.

In Lyon the weavers recognized that these difficult conditions had at first weighed on silk workers, alone, but now they plagued small merchants and manufacturers too. They foresaw that the inevitable result of the present system of free competition was the crushing of all the weak by the strong, the establishment of monopolies; in short, the establishment of a "new feudalism" ensuring its domination through capital and industrial power.

Their analysis of the concentration of wealth, as we described above, was correct. But the analogy with feudalism was misleading. Capitalism was a new system of oppression based on a money economy operating in the free market. In the Lyon silk industry it adopted traditional sex-roles to further exploit workers. During the thirties, silk manufacturers learned from the master craftsmen that it was possible to employ women at the looms as the masters often employed their own wives. They also learned from the family workshop that women should not be paid for their work. They extended this sytem to the convent-workshops which they financed. Here the women worked, received food and shelter, as in the family workshop, and only a few centimes per year to prevent their running away. In the silk factories where manufacturers did not provide food or shelter, they paid the women one franc a day to make sure they would be both able and obliged to return to work each morning.

Because they were vulnerable both as women--who could be burdened with children to support, and as workers--who had no resources to fall back on, the *canutes* who emerged in the 1840's were perfectly exploitable. Employers would have ceased to employ men altogether if it were not for the skill required in weaving. It required several decades to train enough women to fill all the weaving jobs previously held by men. Employers also had a vested interest in maintaining some superior experienced craftsmen to weave special luxury fabrics. They also required the use of some family workshops thus they set up several institutions in the thirties and forties to ensure the survival of some master craftsmen and their family workshops.

The Caisse des Prêts, created by Royal Edict on May 9, 1832, was the first of these institutions, partially funded by the national government, which contributed 25,000 francs, the rest funded by Lyonese private investors.[50] It was administered by a council whose members were chosen by the Conseil des Prud'hommes, a body made up of merchants and master weavers charged with settling industrial disputes, and the Chamber of Commerce of Lyon. Only master weavers who were married and were established in their own workshops for one year were eligible for loans. The Caisse lent 50 francs for each loom owned by the master, at 5% interest.[51] The debt was inscribed on the master's books and one-eighth of all his future wages went towards payment of the debt.

Though the early thirties were relatively prosperous for the weavers, approximately 1500 of them requested loans each year. By December 1835, 440,505 francs had been loaned, indicating the commitment of local investors to keep masters and their workshops afloat. The loans represented an average of only 83 francs per master which indicated that those requesting loans had only one or two looms to work with. Despite the wages which were withheld to repay the loans, only 33,156 francs were paid back by December 1835, less than 10% of the money loaned, which pointed to the low level of wages. In 1837, when American markets were closed to French silks, a 25% increase in the number of loans requested was registered, showing once again the importance of foreign markets to the silk industry in Lyon.

Journeymen weavers and masters who had not yet repaid 75% of their loan from the Caisse were permitted to borrow from the Mont de Piété, which provided credit only with the deposit of a guarantee as collateral. The guarantee most often used in these pawn shops was clothing and since the amount of money loaned was far greater than the amount repaid, most items given as collateral were never returned. Interest on loans were higher here than at the Caisse. Loans of less than 1,000 francs earned 12% interest for the creditors who were local Lyonese merchants; on loans between 1,000 and 2,000 francs, the interest was 8%. Since the average loan was only 100 francs,[52] it is likely that weavers used the money to pay for food and shelter during periods of stress than to accumulate enough capital to set themselves up in new workshops. This, naturally, suited the goals of the business community in Lyon who wanted to help some of the masters survive, but they were not willing to foot the bill to create new family workshops.

A third institution--the Bureau de Bienfaisance--was established to deal directly with the silk workers who failed to survive on their own. Its function was to distribute food, clothing and money to the needy. During the period 1842-7 the number of indigents helped by the Bureau exceeded 20,000 per year. [53] In 1844, for example, 51,864 francs-worth of food, 9,483 francs-worth of clothing and 194,157 francs in cash was dispensed by the Bureau. The Bureau was another means by which the bourgeois merchants kept enough of their skilled labor forces alive so that they could be called back to the workshops when the demand for silk increased, while simultaneously protecting the entrepreneurs from urban riots.

Workers whose needs exceeded the dole from the Bureau and who resorted to begging were arrested and placed in the Dépôt de Mendicité, the Lyonese equivalent of the English poor house. Here workshops were organized and the *canuts* and *canutes,* primarily old and sick from years of work in the silk industry, were again put to work, to pay for the minimum of food, clothing and shelter they received. The Dépôt, built for 150 workers generally housed 300. The inmates were surrounded by guards and were not permitted to leave unless they were claimed by their families. [54]

The Dépôt was too small to take care of all the vagrant workers in Lyon. In times of crisis when the numbers of beggars increased, the Municipal Council voted additional sums to be distributed to the needy to prevent widespread starvation. In 1842, for example, when 15-18,000 looms were idle, the Council voted immediate distribution of 30,000 francs to the needy. This sum, generous as it seemed to some, represented less than one franc per person, hardly enough to survive on through the crisis. [55] Yet large numbers of workers in Lyon did not die of starvation, even during the big crisis of 1845-47. The reason for their survival is due to a clever idea on the part of the Lyonese silk entrepreneurs who by the mid-forties not only wanted to preserve their skilled work force but who had also become increasingly fearful of urban riots. These businessmen arranged for secret doles to thousands of workers by neighborhood butchers and bakers. Assistants in the local shops reported that more than half the working class in Lyon were receiving free bread, meat, charcoal and medicine. [56] The secret charity was successful because the workers preferred to refrain from registering with the Bureau de Bienfaisance as they were ashamed to be unemployed or unable to support themselves. The manufacturers encouraged this sense of pride because they feared riots if all needy workers registered for official charity. It was estimated that secret charity made up about half of the total charity given out in Lyon.[57]

By employing this system of doles and hiring increasing numbers of *canutes* weaving simple silks in convent-workshops to slowly replace the master craftsmen weaving luxury silks in family workshops, the new silk industrialists managed to maintain and often to expand their businesses throughout the unsteady forties. At the same time male weavers never ceased to demand higher wages for themselves, in a vain attempt to maintain their artisan way of life. In all their numerous plans for reorganizing labor, *Organization du Travail* was the slogan of a worker weekly in the mid-forties, they unwittingly obliged the industrialists by never including the growing number of women workers.

While the artisans looked back nostalgically to the golden age of the family workshop, the bourgeoisie were busy harnessing the energy of the new technology and finance. The position of women workers became confused in this push and pull of the early industrial revolution. The segregation of work place from family and home was accompanied by loud protests about the role of women in the family, an issue which was already under hot debate by Saint-Simonians, feminists and more traditional voices of the bourgeoisie. Though the *canutes* in Lyon were the first silk workers to leave the family workshops to seek employment in larger workshops and factories, they were encouraged by their husbands, by feminists, by the schools and the church, to see themselves as only temporary workers, whose primary function was to be wives and mothers.

Chapter II

WOMEN'S WORK: EMPLOYMENT AND UNEMPLOYMENT

In the 1830's and 1840's all three of the processes involved in silk production--removing the silk from the cocoon, twisting the thread, and weaving--were modernized by the introduction of new machinery, some of which required steam and steam power. Many of the improved machines--reels, unwinders, warpers, and Jacquard looms, were set up in large workshops or factories owned by silk manufacturers. Seventy percent of the employees in these early factories were women called *canutes,* [1] who performed traditional tasks with new tools, and in new places, under new supervision.

Traditionally, silk worms were raised by peasant women in the Rhône valley. They nourished the worms on mulberry leaves, from trees tended by their husbands, then suffocated the worms by exposing them to the sun, to prevent them from turning into butterflies. Finally, they pulled the silk filaments from the cocoon and reeled them onto a skein. They did their work at home or in a small workshop owned by one or more of the farmers. [2]

The exact procedure was tiring and painful, but no more so than other farm duties. The woman placed her cocoons in a basin of water which was heated by a small charcoal stove standing underneath the basin. She brought the temperature of the water almost to the boiling point and in this way dissolved the gummy substance (sericin) which held the cocoon together. Then she thrust her hand into the water, seized one end of the silk filament and pulled it from the dissolving cocoon. After unwinding the filament, she extracted a second, third and fourth filament from the water and unwound each of them. She attached these filaments to each other by pressing them together; the remnants of the sericin kept them from separating. The woman then wound the resultant strand of silk onto a reel which she kept turning by hand or foot movement. [3]

The working conditions of the peasant women who pulled, reeled and tended the stove, were poor. They sat in a cramped position, bending over the basin and reaching down to the stove. The smoke from the stove and the steam were harmful to their lungs. The hot water scalded their fingers. [4] But peasant women tended the cocoons only a few hours a day; they spent the rest of the day doing other chores which involved more vigorous exercise [5] and they had plenty of fresh country air to breathe.

The traditional method of pulling and reeling silk continued throughout the first half of the nineteenth century, but gradually more and more pulling and reeling factories, called *filatures,* which used steam to heat the basins, were constructed in and near Lyon. [6] Silk entrepreneurs were eager to improve the quality of the raw silk produced on the farm, which was often poor. The woman who had to tend a stove while pulling and reeling was unable to do either job well. Her stove frequently gave out smoke that was bad for the delicate fibers of the silk, and it often operated irregularly so that the temperature of the water in the basin was not uniform.

The factories which opened in Lyon and its suburbs employed between 50 and 100 peasant women (*fileuses*) who came from the surrounding rural communities. [7] These women worked full-time at the factories. In the forties this meant that they worked 14 to 16 hours each day reeling, less the time for three meals. Sundays were the only holidays. [8] This exhausting work schedule alternated with days, weeks, and even months of unemployment.

In the reeling factories a precise division of labor was designed to extract the maximum work from the employees. Growing and feeding the worms continued to be done on the farms, but all other tasks were specialized in the factory. The first job was to suffocate the worms, usually, by means of a steam oven. After that, the women in charge removed the cocoons from the ovens and placed them individually on large trays stored in well-ventilated rooms where they dried. The drying process took three months and women were employed to turn the cocoons to speed the evaporation of the water.[9] This lengthy procedure also allowed the cocoons to lose their stench.

Next the cocoons were brought to the women who specialized in pulling the silk fibers from the dried cocoon. These women sat in front of earthenware or copper basins which were full of water. They tossed their cocoons into the basins, bringing the water to a very high temperature by turning a knob which released swirling steam into the basin. Then, they beat the cocoons with a small briar brush gently increasing the rotation of the cocoons in the water. The purpose of this movement was to loosen the top layers of the cocoon which were made of inferior silk.[10] When this was accomplished, the women thrust their hands into the water and pulled out the filaments of high quality silk, lowering the temperature in the basin to 138°F quickly so as not to weaken the cocoon too rapidly. After removing the better silk filaments, they also removed the inferior silk which was put aside for making mixed textiles. The superior silk filaments were taken by other women who pressed several of them together to form a strand. These strands were then given to yet other women who reeled them onto a skein.

The reeling techniques were greatly improved during the first half of the nineteenth century. Technical innovations in the construction of the reels enabled the reeler to cross the strands of silk back and forth in order to make them stronger. Steam was used as a source of power to turn the reels so that the reeler could give all her attention to the silk strands.

All of the women employed in the reeling factory--those who steamed and dried the cocoons, those who pulled the silk filaments from the cocoons, those who pressed the filaments together to form strands, and those who reeled the strands onto skeins--worked under the observation of a foreman, who was always a man. This was an extension of male authority into a process in which traditionally silk producing women were self-governed. The foreman's job was to make sure that the women did not lapse into periods of inattention or slow down the pace of their work. For his overseeing his was paid double or triple the wages of the working women plus sexual favors which we will discuss below.[11]

The new machines, the division of labor, and the vigilant foreman, produced silk strands of higher and more uniform quality than any made on the farms. The use of steam enabled the women to maintain an even temperature in their basins and to separate the superior silk from the inferior fragments. The new reeling mechanisms eliminated irregularities from the silk strands.[12] Pleased with the product, the Lyonese silk manufacturers continued to invest money in reeling factories,[13] and were able to supply the new mills (*moulinages*) with increasing numbers of skeins.

These skeins of silk strands or raw silk were very ductile, stretching 14% to 20%.[14] They were not ready to be woven because washing them dissolved the residual sericin which held the individual strands together.[15] In order to produce a thread which could withstand dyeing and weaving, the raw silk was milled. Like pulling and reeling, milling was traditionally a woman's job. In fact it was often done by the same women who did pulling and reeling earlier in the season, both in the primitive home processing and in factories.[16]

In the forties, small workshops of eight to ten peasant women (*moulinières*) working near their homes were replaced by workshops which employed thirty to forty women workers in the larger villages and towns.[17] Unlike the old shops where the women brought their own crude tools, the new shops used steam power to run machinery owned by the employer. Like the pulling and reeling factories they operated fourteen to sixteen hours each day, and subjected their employees to strict division of labor under the supervision of a foreman.

In the mill there were three specific tasks: first the skeins of raw silk were soaked in an oil-based emulsion for about eight hours at 80°F, softening the residual sericin and making it more pliable; then, the skeins were individually dried; finally, the strands were unwound from the skeins onto spools or bobbins. The new machines made it possible to wind the strands onto the bobbins with a rapid reciprocating motion, so as to be able to lay the thread in a crossing diamond-like pattern on the bobbin. This process of crossing the strands over each other was repeated several times; several strands twisted around each other--the exact number of twists depending on the eventual use of the thread--produced a single thread ready to be dyed.[18]

In addition to the pullers, reelers, and millers, there was one more group of women who worked in the preliminary aspects of silk production, these were the women (*bourretaires*) who prepared waste silk thread from defective cocoons, the inferior parts of good cocoons, and the thread which tore or knotted during reeling, milling or weaving. Spinning jennies developed for cotton and wool were adapted to preparing waste silk to be woven with cotton and woolen into mixed textiles. As we noted earlier, the chief center of preparing waste silk was Lyon, where it was used to weave plush, imitation furs, and Mecklenburg velvets.[19]

The waste silk workers were employed in underground or ground level workshops whose windows were tightly closed. The air was very humid and dust from the silk particles circulated constantly around them.[20] They endured the same long hours, and the same foremen as the pullers, reelers, and millers.

The silk manufacturers, who needed higher quality and greater quantities of silk thread to feed the Jacquard looms which were capable of producing 25% more silk each day than the old models, saw only the positive aspects of the mechanization of the preliminary processes of silk production. For their women employees, though, there were many negative aspects. We have already mentioned the long hours, the monotony of repeating the same task all day long and the exploitation of some women by unscrupulous foremen. In addition to all these, the women suffered from severe health hazards related to their specific jobs. In the pulling and reeling factories they constantly inhaled the overpowering stench caused by the putrified chrysalis, a stench which clung to their clothing after work.[21] Those who were engaged in pulling the silk fibers from the cocoon had pain-riddled fingers from the near boiling water in their basins. Despite frequent immersion of their fingers in cold water or red wine which they kept beside their basins,[22] they all suffered from abscesses and sores under their fingernails. The millers who soaked the skeins and those who dried them also emerged with damaged hands. Those who reeled the silk strands onto the skeins and those who twisted the strands onto the bobbins had to strain their eyes watching the strands crisscrossing fifteen hours a day, making sure that none of them broke or tangled. Women who combed the waste silk succumbed very young to lung disease, especially tuberculosis. Chronic eye disease, asthma, pneumonia, and blood spitting were common among these women. 23

Generally speaking, working conditions in these early factories were responsible for many premature deaths and illnesses. Tuberculosis accounted for 20% of the deaths in Lyon, and was much more common among young women than men, because women had sedentary jobs in which they were exposed to the unhealthful conditions much longer than men and because they were paid less and were worse nourished. 24 No ventilation was permitted in the workshops and factories (with the exception of the drying room in the reeling factories) for fear of damaging the delicate and expensive silk. As a result, the women were always covered with silk dust, their pores were plugged with it and they developed persistent skin diseases which healed only during periods of long unemployment.

Accidents were frequent occurrences on the job, but there were no long term provisions for workers who caught their hair or clothes in a machine, or whose hands were mutilated by immersion in boiling water. A good employer often paid the doctor bill and sometimes the workers took up a collection to help with the immediate expenses, but after that, the accident victim was abandoned. 25

In addition to the health and accident hazards, were the changes in consciousness resulting from work in a mill. Women who worked in the *filatures* saw themselves as part of a larger process in which there was a hierarchy of experts (foremen). In this setting their work had a machine-like functionality; the actions of the individual *canute* were tied in as an intrinsic part of the machine process. This led to the segregation of work from private life. 26 Not only was the work place cut off from the family workshop, but the consciousness of the worker reflected this segregation as well. Home became a center for intensified emotional life, while on the job the *canute* was reduced to a component of the machine process.

Women were also involved in the next phase of the industry preparing the thread for the loom. Their work was as tedious and as long as that of the women discussed above, but it was not as physically painful, nor as unpleasant. Frequently, they were employed by a master weaver and worked in his small family workshop for two or three days at a time. But, in the forties, many of these women experienced a change of employers and of place of work. Those whose work involved new or expensive machinery moved to large workshops or factories owned by silk merchants who employed them at a daily wage. La Sauvagère, situated on the banks of the Saône, was such a factory. It employed four hundred to five hundred men and women and produced all kinds of silk specializing in mixtures of silk, cotton and wool in multicolored patterns. [27] Merchants who couldn't afford to construct new buildings for their business financed workshops within the convents of Lyon. [28]

The master weavers and their family workshops, though suffering great financial strain, were not replaced by factories and convent-workshops all at once. In fact, throughout the period more people were hired by artisans than by factory bosses. [29] Usually a master weaver received an order from a merchant for a specific quantity of a particular pattern of silk. The merchant often brought the weaver the milled thread to work with or advanced him money to buy thread. The weaver then hired a woman quality controller (*metteuse*) who was in charge of separating the milled thread into bundles destined to be used for warp thread and bundles for woof. [30] The controller came to the weaver's workshop or worked at home on a simple device which was not improved during the forties. The tool had two sets of horizontal wooden bars (see Fig. 1) on which she draped the milled thread. She stroked the bundles and increased the regularity of the threads to differentiate between warp and woof quality.

When the controller finished, the thread was sent to the dyers who colored it according to the specifications of the weavers. Dyeing in this period was exclusively a man's job so we will not go into the details of the process. Suffice it to say that the silk was dyed on skeins [31] which

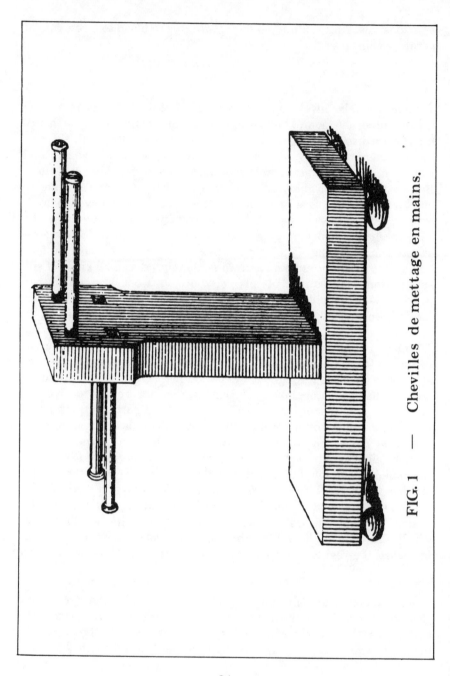

FIG. 1 — Chevilles de mettage en mains.

were then returned to the weaver who hired another woman, also called a reeler (*devideuse*), who removed the thread from the skeins, careful to maintain the separation between warp and woof.

The reeler could work in the weaver's workshop or at her own home, unwinding skeins onto bobbins on simple machines. Most of the unwinding of woof thread was done in this manner. But, unwinding of warp thread was usually done in specialized workshops, owned by a silk merchant. [32] The reason for this was the *devidoir de Lyon* (see Fig. 2), a machine which came into use in the eighteenth century, making it possible for a single reeler to unwind skeins onto four bobbins simultaneously, increasing her output per hour and ensuring the evenness of the thread on all four bobbins. By the mid-1840's, a machine with twelve bobbins, operated by a foot pedal, was widely in use in Lyon. [33]

The silk thread which was to be used for the woof was sent from the reeler to another woman worker, the woof winder (*canneteuse*). The job of the latter was to remove the thread from the bobbins and wind equal amounts of thread onto a specified number of small cylinders (usually made out of cane) which were then ready to be placed in the weaver's shuttle. The woof winder strove to maintain an equal number of threads at a uniform tension on the cylinders so that the woof would unwind easily. [34] The woof winder often worked in the weaver's workshop on a relatively simple machine (see Fig. 3). She turned the larger wheel pulling the thread off the bobbin (2) and distributing it onto the four cylinders (1).

The other bobbins of thread, which were destined to be used for the warp, were sent from the reeler to another woman worker, the warper (*ourdisseuse*), who prepared the warp for the weaver. Her job was to place a predetermined number of threads of equal length parallel to one another on a frame. She had to make sure that there were no empty spaces, no broken threads, and that each thread was equally taut. The threads had to remain in place to avoid tangling which would have made weaving impossible. [35]

The Jacquard loom made it possible to weave more complicated patterns, requiring more and more threads (thousands) in the warp. In

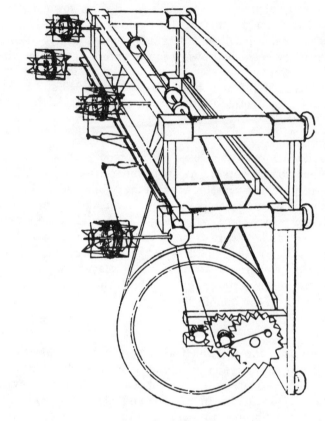

FIG.2 — Ancien dévidoir de Lyon à quatre guidres.

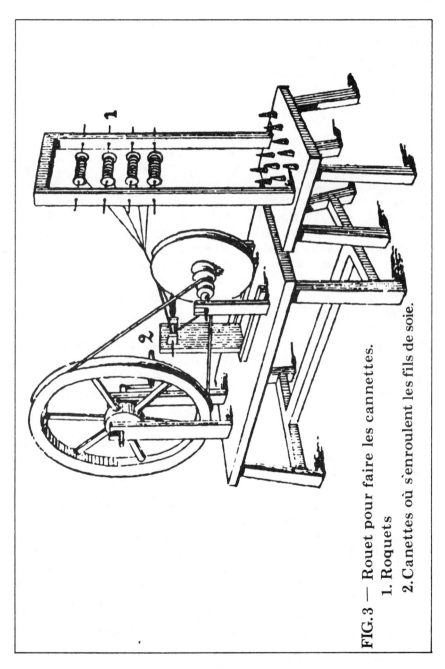

FIG.3 — Rouet pour faire les cannettes.
1. Roquets
2. Canettes où s'enroulent les fils de soie.

27

order to perform her job, the warper had to separate the bobbins into groups of 40 each (*musette*), and then warp each group separately on a warping machine (*ourdissoir*) (see Fig. 4). If, for example, the warper received an order to prepare a warp composed of 4,000 bobbins having a length of 100 meters, she subdivided the number of bobbins into 100 groups and warped each one separately.[36]

The warpers sent their finished work to another woman, the warp finisher, who was in charge of placing the groups (*musettes*) in the width they would have in the final fabric. This worker was usually a woman, called a *plieuse*, but sometimes the job was performed by men (*plieurs*), too. The fact that men and women were both hired to do the same task perhaps reflected the lack of a traditional sex-identification with warp finishing. Since it was a relatively new task, tied to the capabilities of the Jacquard loom, there was no traditional sex-identification with the task.[37] The finishers used a simple machine (see Fig. 5) to wind all the threads onto the cylinder of the loom and then brought the cylinder to the weaver. This machine was often kept in the weaver's workshop during our period.[38]

The actual process of weaving was the most complicated of all tasks in the early manufacture of silk. Every woven fabric was the result of the combination of warp and woof. The threads of the warp had to be far enough apart from each other to allow the woof to pass through. In non-figured weaves such as satin and velvet, which were increasingly woven by women in our period,[39] a heald-harness loom was used. The object of the heald-harness was to lift or depress warp threads so that a passage was formed through which the shuttle containing the woof could be passed.

Figured fabrics--those ornamented with a woven design--continued to be woven almost exclusively by men, who used either the old draw-loom or the new Jacquard loom. With the draw-loom a weaver required the help of an assistant who controlled the figure-harness either from the top or the side of the loom. The weaver sat in front of the loom working both with foot treadles and with his hands to beat the woof into the fabric. The Jacquard loom (see Plate 1), invented in 1801, removed the need for an assistant by arranging for all the movements to be worked from one seat at the loom. Though the Jacquard loom was

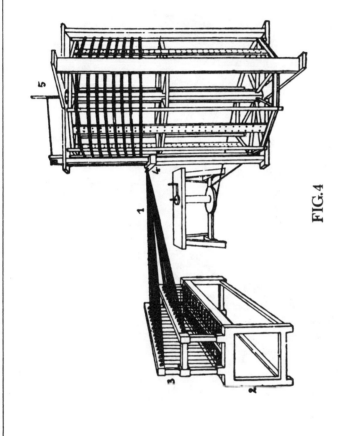

FIG.4

1. Musette s'ourdissant. — 2.Cantre
3. Rangée d'anneaux en vorre correspondant aux brôches.
4. Ourdissoir. — 5.Axe autour duquel s'enroule la corde qui soulève le plot.

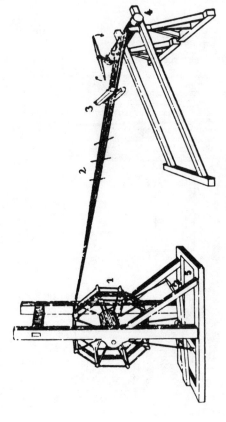

FIG.5   Pliage.

1.Tambour. — 2.Verges. — 3.Rasteau. — 4.Ensouple.
5.Bascule de serrage du tambour.

Plate 1

introduced rapidly in France--by 1812 there were 11,000--both types were still widely used through 1870. [40]

As we noted earlier, the reelers, warpers, and weavers were regimented by the same long hours, monotonous tasks and foreman's supervision as the women who prepared the raw silk. All of the women workers in our period suffered from the dry, dusty workshops or factories in which they worked. The windows in these workshops were always sealed to prevent the air from affecting the color or weight of the delicate silk. [41] Women who worked at the loom suffered additional physical discomfort. They often had hunched backs and concave chests, a posture resulting from their position at the loom. They had no firm support for their feet, which were alternately raised and lowered in operating the treadles. They had to depend on the muscles of their backs for a fulcrum. Further, the cylinder on which the finished fabric was rolled reached the weavers' stomachs so that they had to constantly bend over it in their work. [42]

Silk manufacturers knew that there was a large labor supply and that they did not have to be overly concerned about the physical health of their employees. After all, backaches did not prevent the *canutes* from doing their jobs. The manufacturers did seem more concerned with the spiritual (or psychological) health of their workers. To combat their feelings of meaninglessness or anomie created by the specialization of each step in the production, the *canutes* were encouraged to find temporary refuge in religion which emphasized a suffering and resigned Virgin with whom they could identify. A small statue of the Virgin was installed in most workshops and the women were directed to decorate the statue (at their own expense) and to recite prayers to the Virgin upon entering and leaving. [43]

But the consciousness of the *canutes* was primarily influenced by the terms of their employment and their frequent periods of unemployment. We know little enough about working class culture as a whole, especially about the women of the working class and their particular culture. But we can isolate some concrete manifestations of working women's consciousness in mid-nineteenth century Lyon. First prostitution was widely (figures follow) adopted by working women who were unemployed or unable to earn enough from their regular employment in order to survive; second, some women workers turned to political and unionizing activity especially during the aftermath of the spring 1848 revolution.

The evidence for widespread prostitution begins with contemporaries' observations. Villermé noted the prevalence of sexual compliance being virtually a job requirement in some cases. [44] Thouvenin also recalled foremen who boasted that they had forced themselves on twenty of their women workers by offering to increase their wages if they didn't resist and threatening to reduce them if they refused. Others boasted of never having been refused by any of their women. Eighteen-year-old mothers working in the *filatures* with two or three fatherless children made these boasts credible. [45] The liberal *Le Precurseur* of 24 October 1831 summed it up: "The punctuality and skillfulness of women workers are not rewarded if they are not combined with the grace of youth and followed by odious compromises."

Male workers also reported on the prevalence of prostitution. Joseph Benoit recorded in his memoirs arriving in Lyon in winter of 1829, and having nothing to eat nor a place to sleep for two days until he met a woman from his village "who had been forced by circumstances to lead an irregular life." [46] She kept an apartment which was frequented by women who needed a temporary refuge and preferred prostitution to starvation. The women who came to this apartment were poor women, unemployed, without any resources. They used prostitution to pay for the things they needed to stay alive. According to Benoit, most of the women left this apartment as soon as they found another job. It would seem that prostitution is further evidence of the *canutes'* ability to sever life from work; to treat themselves as anonymous workers. [47]

Not all were forced or pushed into sexual relations. Some undoubtedly initiated these relations for their own reasons. One indication of women's sense of newly acquired power resulting from their increasing awareness of the marketability of their bodies was the unique incident of a prostitutes' organization in 1848--recorded in the police reports as L'Affaire Jourdan. [48] Madame Jourdan, who used to run a cabaret in LaGuillotiere (suburb of Lyon) where "public girls" gathered, was accused of organizing meetings of up to 1500 women. The police claimed that she profited from the general turmoil of the revolution by gathering women to preach to them disorderly and immoral ideas. At one of these meetings she urged her audience of women to confront Arago, the provisional government's representative in Lyon, with a demand to extend credit to them to open a workshop. Some money was provided, and a workshop was opened. The methods of operation for this workshop were illustrative of use of their special power. Madame Jourdan instructed *pretty* young *canutes* to entice wealthy merchants to their shop, to allow relationships to develop, and then to demand marriage or high compensation. [49] Madame Jourdan was able to collect in several cases; she kept a share of the money for herself and divided the rest equally among the *canutes*.

The scandals emanating from her workshop as well as the frequent meetings of women workers brought the attention of the police to her case. She was asked to cease her activity. She refused. The police claimed to receive reports that "people" were threatening to hurt her, to destroy her home, etc., thus for her own good they arrested her. She was released after agreeing not to hold any more meetings and to close down her workshop.

The activities of prostitutes become all the more important for this study when it becomes evident that many of the women accused of sex-related crimes--prostitution, seduction, indecent exposure, immodest behavior--were silk workers. Among a group of 305 women arrested during September and October, 1848, there was no significant difference (using chi square analysis) between women who had no skills and those who were silk workers in arrests for sex-related crimes. [50] (See Appendix B, Chart 1.)

Further, it is clear that a significant element which pushed women into these crimes was not having a place to live. That is, using the same analysis, comparing women who had a home address with those who reported none, the latter group were more likely to be arrested for sex-related crimes. (See Appendix B, Chart 2.) This analysis supports the earlier description by Benoit. In sum, prostitution and sex-related crimes were committed by single women (married women and widows were arrested primarily for begging), [51] who may or may not have come from the countryside (no significant difference was found with regard to sex-related crimes for women of rural and Lyonese origins), [52] who were likely to be homeless and also likely to fall into the 21 to 30-year-old age group. (See Appendix B, Chart 3.)

Another manifestation of women's consciousness was their adoption of physical force as a weapon to improve their living conditions. Their ability to organize, to see the identity of their interests, was possible now that they saw people not only as friends, neighbors, family members but also as part of the working class. In early March of 1848 women concerned with winning higher wages and shorter hours for themselves joined groups and circulated in the reeling workshops which were still operating and physically threatened anyone who did not demand a raise. [53] Later in the month, a corps of 400 women gathered in the courtyard of the Saint Pierre Palace and put on a military demonstration. They divided into brigades, each one commanded by a woman leader. They marched to the beat of drums and performed a flag ceremony. Men workers and soldiers who had come to stare, soon joined their ranks. Six hundred of them then marched to the prisons, opened them, and freed all the prisoners. [54]

Next an army of women marched to the Prefecture of Police and presented Arago with a demand to establish National Workshops for women. Arago had already opened National Workshops for the men silk workers and ordered them to weave 120,000 scarves and 43,000 flags for the new republic. The workshop for *canutes* was opened shortly thereafter on the Place du Petit-College. It took in 200 workers, providing them with a place to live and a small wage. [55]

The tradition of mutual-aid was expressed by women workers as well as by men in the aftermath of the 1848 revolutions. At the end of the year, when winter cold and lack of work overtook the silk workers, many cooperatives--both producer and consumer cooperatives--were formed in Lyon, several of them were restricted to women workers and confronted their specific problems. One producer cooperative included forewomen, child care services, and paid women enough to support themselves.

This is evidence that women who worked in silk factories in mid-century began to develop a new consciousness, one which was increasingly different from that of artisan weavers, employed or unemployed. The problems of sexual exploitation, prostitution, unwanted pregnancies and children, who had to be cared for, were unique to women workers. Their growing consciousness of themselves as wage earners was modified, however, by the advice of feminists and socialists, priests and teachers, and by family tradition.

Chapter III

THE MEDIA'S MESSAGE: FEMINIST AND SOCIALIST MYTHS

The city of Lyon had many newspapers reporting on the economic and political scene in the 1830's, ranging from the conservative *Courrier de Lyon*, to the radical *L'Echo des Travailleurs* with the bourgeois *Le Censeur* and the master weavers' *L'Echo de la Fabrique* completing the spectrum. (See Appendix C for explanation of journal titles.) It even had one paper --*Le Papillon*--addressed to the *dames*, the ladies, of Lyon. Founded in June 1832 by a society of "men of the world, artists, and men of letters," it was a journal devoted only to literature, music, painting, theater, and fashion. It promised in the prospectus to be as light and airy as the wings of a butterfly and its multicolored issues were designed to please the eye.[1]   But Lyon did not have any journal addressed to working women. In 1833 Eugenie Niboyet decided to fill that gap by founding a feminist journal addressed to all women.[2]

Niboyet, born Eugenie Mouchon in 1800, was the daughter of a doctor from Montpellier in southern France, and the granddaughter of a Swiss pastor. Both of her parents were of liberal persuasion and Protestant faith. Niboyet's childhood was spent in the cult of equality and Bonapartist glory which followed the revolution. While she was studying at home her brothers gained many honors in the Grande Armée. At the age of 20 she married a Protestant lawyer who came from Lyon.

After a youth spent amongst pastors, officers, doctors and lawyers, Niboyet found the life of a bourgeois housewife (she had one son, Paulin) confining. She soon became interested in prison reform, the abolition of the death penalty, Owenists and Saint-Simonism. In Paris, she became the Secretary-General of the Society for Christian Morality, presided over by LaRochefoucauld-Liancourt. There she met the daughter of Lafayette and Mme de Lamartine. In 1831 she became the chief of the Saint-Simonian chapter of the fourth arrondissement of Paris. [3] She adopted many of the Saint-Simonian principles about women, especially the idea that women, far from being burdened with the original sin, should be man's guide through life. [4]

Meanwhile, all around her in Paris journals for women were being launched. The most radical, *La Femme Libre*, was founded in August 1832 by a group of women workers who put together their modest resources to establish a newspaper to work for the emancipation of women. Their motto: "Liberty for women, liberty for the people, by a new organization of household and industry" was indicative of their general conviction that women would only be happy after a total revolution of society. [5] The contributors to this journal were women like Jeanne Deroin, a seamstress who taught herself to read, and later became a teacher, and Suzanne Voilquin, a seamstress who became a midwife and later practiced her profession in Russia. In the two years of its existence, these women changed the name of their newspaper several times. *La Femme de l'Avenir, La Femme Nouvelle, L'Apostolat des Femmes, La Tribune des Femmes*, were all attempts to focus attention on their radical theme of social change.

That same year a different type of woman's journal was founded in Paris, *Le Journal des Femmes*. [6] Fanny Richomme edited it with a more conservative stance for almost five years. Her goal was twofold: to make women apt in the duties of companion and mother; and to publicize literature written by women. Unlike *La Femme Libre*, this woman's journal restricted its audience by charging 2.50 francs per issue, compared to 15 centimes per issue of the former. *Le Journal des Femmes* used luxurious paper and print and its contributors, including Georges Sand and Mme Victor Hugo, were prestigious.

In September 1833, Madeline Sirey, a niece of Mirabeau, founded yet another journal for women, *La Mère de Famille*. [7] As the title suggested this journal emphasized woman's role in the family. It was directed to her moral, religious, and literary interests, as well as to the questions of economics and domestic hygiene.

Eugenie Niboyet was influenced by all of these periodicals, and when she accompanied her husband back to Lyon in 1833 she launched *Le Conseiller des Femmes*. Niboyet was convinced that there was room in Lyon for a feminist journal, one dedicated to the advancement of all women, rather than for the mere pleasure of the leisured women who read the *Papillon*. The *Conseiller* was relatively inexpensive--ten francs per year for 52 issues, compared to twenty-four francs for the *Papillon* [8] --indicating her goal of reaching all women, not just the wealthy.

The goals of *Le Conseiller*, reflecting Niboyet's Saint-Simonian leanings, were stated in a prospectus issued in October 1833. "Convinced that it is the duty of our sex to temper the character of men, we have conceived the project of founding in Lyon, a populous city where women are in the majority in the workshops and in the businesses, a practical journal having for its goal the amelioration of women's conditions in all social ranks." [9] The prospectus announced sections on health care: nursing, weaning, teeth cleaning; on general knowledge: grammar, history, geography, biography of famous women; on fashion with the purpose of improving taste; on theater for its moral lessons; and on household management. [10] Each of these sections was addressed specifically to bourgeois or to working women.

The Lyonese press was generally quick to respond to the prospectus. On October 27th, the *Echo de la fabrique* devoted an article to the appearance of the new journal. They applauded Niboyet's resolution to start a journal where the voices of women would be heard on the theme of social change. "Women," they affirmed, "can no longer remain estranged from the important social issues which face us." [11] The *Echo* reproduced a long citation from the prospectus and informed their readers where to buy the newspaper. The *Papillon* also approved of Niboyet's effort to launch another woman's journal. It congratulated her attempts "to instruct, to moralize, and to advance a sex which to this day has been closed in a sphere too narrow for its development." [12] They too, published a long section from the prospectus. The simultaneous acclaim from the artisan's press and a ladies' journal should not lead to confusion. It was an early indication that male craftsmen and bourgeois women frequently agreed on the proper place for working women--the home.

The silence of other journals and the condemnation by the *Reparateur*--on religious grounds [13] --were in keeping with the pervasive attitudes about women. The physical and intellectual superiority of men was the conventional wisdom of the day. Specifically, it was widely believed that men had two or three ounces more brain matter than women. [14] These feelings were codified into law in the Code Civil of 1804, most of which remained in force throughout the century. There were over 200 articles of this law which pertained directly to the status of women. According to one, "persons declared unfit according to the law were minors, ex-convicts, and married women."[15] Another held that a husband had the right to prohibit his wife from working and at the same time was the administrator of his wife's estate and entitled to dispose of it without her consent. [16] Another made it clear that, "The husband owes protection to the wife and the wife obedience to the husband."[17]

The *Conseiller* was convinced that this attitude could not be changed without rich and poor women uniting to work for their collective freedom. In a stirring article in the first issue, Louise Maignaud urged an end to class antagonism among women. She specifically wished to do away with the anxiety of bourgeois wives who feared that their husbands were being led astray by promiscuous poor women. In short she hoped to unify "virtuous women" and "women of easy virtue." Her appeal for sisterhood became a central theme for the journal.

> *Women will not really be strong until they become in good faith the friend of their own sex; that is the first virtue of men that they should try to imitate if they do not want to be eternal slaves to men. An esprit de corps is lacking to women; and that is the cause of the birth of their dependence and their slavery. The lack of harmony between women will always be fatal to their progress.* [18]

This appeal for unity masked the underlying intention of the editors of the *Conseiller* which was to carry the values of the male bourgeoisie--self-discipline, hard work for delayed rewards, and order--to women. Not surprisingly these values could not be followed in the same way by rich and poor women. Recognizing that these two groups had very different life styles, the *Conseiller* published stories and articles specifically designed to illustrate and solve the problems of each.

Maignaud deplored the fact that for her contemporaries: "Love is but an episode in the life of a man, but it is the entire life of a woman." [19] She diagnosed the crucial issue for bourgeois women as their poor education which led them to a life of dependence on the constant affection of their husbands and consequently to unhappiness. Women, she continued, were not inherently limited to one interest in life; on the contrary, when this occurred, it was the result of poor social planning. [20] Women were restricted from learning anything else; they could not study sciences and the arts, and that was why their only interest was love. With more liberty women could have--like men--a thousand interests to occupy them. "When women have changed their existence of trinkets for an existence based on more solid things, when, they become more instructed, then love will be no more than an episode in their lives as well," [21] Maignaud asserted. Then women will cease to lead the withered and faded existence they now lead as they inevitably lose the illusions of their youth. In addition, the crime of seduction will be less widespread, because the more enlightened women would be, the more they would know how to defend themselves. The thorny question of the double sexual standard would also be solved by enlarging the sphere of women. In Maignaud's opinion the more enlightened women would become, the more they would know how to defend themselves. Thus the double standard would become inoperative by reducing the number of women who could be seduced.

Another contributor to *Le Conseiller des Femmes*, Madame Sophie Ulliac Dudrezene, explained in a different issue that if women sincerely wanted to change their social conditions, there was only one way to do it: that was to make their young daughters and sisters profit from their bitter experience. [22] Eugenie Niboyet was determined to make a start with the present generation. In the December 21, 1833, issue of *Le Conseiller des Femmes,* she announced a plan to open up a moral and intellectual tribune for women. The members of the society, to be called *l'Athenée*, would have meetings to read works and discuss issues. Each member would pay a fee of 20 francs annually to help purchase a library and books. She gave them until January 15, 1834, to register their membership.

On the 15th they had an organizational meeting and voted for officers. The group continued to meet regularly throughout the year. On March 15, 1834, they published the by-laws of the organization in the

Conseiller des Femmes. The most interesting articles referred to the right of each member to start her own course of study. Meetings were held every two weeks to read to each other their own works, and papers of real interest were to be published in the *Conseiller.* An archivist was charged with keeping all their papers in order and registering each member in order of her entrance in the society. [23]

This remarkable effort in self-education was clearly not designed to overthrow the social patterns of the 1830's but merely to inaugurate some accommodations--to enlarge women's sphere slightly. In an article entitled *Emancipation,* Mme M. D'Invilliers spoke for her colleagues on the *Conseiller des Femmes.* She stated that women should not and did not want to stop being women, that they could progress without denying their sex. The few women who have succeeded in science, the arts, and literature have proved that women were capable of such pursuits. Mme D'Invilliers explained "Open to each woman the career which would be appropriate for her and encourage her intellectual dispositions and you will discover treasures hitherto unknown." [24]

Treating each woman as an individual--rather than as Woman--was an important goal of the *Conseiller.* Recognition that women had individual talents and aptitudes would necessitate an end to the myth that women generally were inferior to men and hence put an end to the narrow confinement restricting women from participating fully in society. Once women were allowed to progress according to their individual talents they would achieve personal well-being, they would no longer languish at home, waiting for their husbands' evening return. They also would become members directly useful to society; one of the areas in which, according to the *Conseiller,* they could be mostly so, was in educating other women. [25]

Not surprisingly they concluded that among women in greatest need of instruction was "la fille du peuple," the poor women, who were treated miserably by social institutions. [26] For them life began with woes as they sucked from their mothers' breasts milk spoiled by poor diet and overwork, and it was through the same hardships that they lived and grew up. Many, as a result, remained skinny, puny little creatures who died after a few miserable years. If they did live, they were quickly obliged to work for their living and could not get any of the school training which in the view of Niboyet and Maignaud was so necessary for their general development. [27] The typical working girl, they believed, reached the age of twelve or thirteen without having learned anything except that she must earn money to pay her own way. That this was a significant difference from their own upbringing was clear. That this gave working women a different consciousness of their own conditions and goals never occurred to the editors of the *Conseiller.*

The *Conseiller* had pinpointed boredom as the chief problem of the bourgeois wife, for the worker's wife they thought it was lack of order and planning. [28] Ironically they wished to "free" their sisters by imposing on them the discipline of methodological and regular work, and the exact and synchronized time-spirit. [29] Elisabeth Celnart contributed an illustrative story, "The Rich Laundress and the Poor Book-Stitcher," to show the tragic results of poor management in a worker family in sharp contrast with the benefits of order and planning. [30]

The laundress began her story this way:

> *I had six women workers, my daughter, and myself*
> *working with satisfying results. My husband was*
> *diligent and thrifty, and worked as a lamp-maker....*
> *As a result we owned a respectable home, on the*
> *fourth floor of Bailleul Street in which we had several*
> *pieces of furniture with marble tops.... (But) My work*
> *made me totally neglect the management of the house-*
> *hold. Busy and eager to make money I forgot that it is*
> *more important for women to save and preserve it. At*
> *meal-time I sent to the fruit man, meat man, and dairy*
> *man for supplies and thus paid top prices and wasted*
> *the time of my workers. I could have avoided such*
> *inconvenience by just going early to the market and*
> *supplying for several days. I also neglected to mend our*
> *clothes; the small holes grew larger and everything*
> *deteriorated. Mealtime was never set, it depended on*
> *the quantity of linen I had to process. Errands delayed*
> *our dinner even more and often we dined at seven*

which caused us stomach troubles and annoyed my husband.

She explained how her husband mumbled, swore, and ended up by staying away from home more and more frequently. Since fights developed when he finally did come home, he shunned his family increasingly. He stopped working hard, made bad friends, and took to drink. As a result, his health deteriorated and he died young.

The laundress was very saddened by her husband's death, but since she still had her beloved daughter and her work she found solace in them. She also had little time for grieving because despite all her hard work she couldn't save any money, could barely pay the rent and extra expenses of winter. Finally, she was forced to go into debt. Moreover, her daughter, Mariette, was almost always sickly. While the lack of order was leading to such disastrous results with the laundress, the opposite qualities were showing their results with their neighbor Françoise, a poor bookstitcher who lived two floors above the laundress.

Françoise was a young widow, left with a small son to care for and no resources. She had to earn and save at the same time as much as possible. Strict order and planning seemed to her the only solution. Upon the death of her husband, Françoise sold her necklace, her lace, and her wedding gown to acquire a little capital which enabled her to purchase potatoes, beans, dry fruit, lard, oil, vinegar, and the other necessities of housekeeping. She bought in bulk to avoid paying extra as well as to avoid wasting time and energy on going up and down six flights every meal-time to shop. Her meals, her sleep, the care of her son, house care, everything was carefully scheduled so that she could always have time to earn money.

She did her best and placed her small savings with a notary who had employed her once before. Her child went to free schools; she drilled his lessons with him while stitching. She inculcated in her son the wisdom of order, good behavior, and education. Paul took advantage of this counsel and at the age of twelve was employed as an errand boy for the bookseller for whom his mother worked. While doing the errands Paul reviewed all he learned in the books he read in his free moments. He watched the printing trade and the book business and every evening would tell his mother the events of his day while helping her to finish her work.

The story continued with Paul and Mariette falling in love, while Paul diligently advanced himself and Mariette fell increasingly ill due to excessive work and poor diet. Despite Mariette's efforts to learn from Françoise how to put her affairs and those of the laundry in order it was too late; she died a young girl, leaving her mother heartbroken and destitute.

Thus, Elisabeth Celnart identified the cause of misery amongst poor women--disorder, which led to illness and death. The remedy for this was to teach women how to manage their affairs, how to plan their time to care for a family and a home. The plot of the story could have been different. Celnart could have shown the laundress prospering and enlarging her business; Mariette could have gone to finishing school and made a good match. But Celnart's message was clear: a mother's preoccupation with business meant disaster for her husband, her child, and ultimately for herself. Françoise was the preferred model--diligent, deferring gratification, and planning her every moment to revolve around her son and her home.

Niboyet and the other writers for the *Conseiller* urged the creation of schools for the poor girls which would educate them and provide a new generation of able wives, mothers, and workers modelled after Françoise. This would also free the mothers of these girls to begin to get their own homes in order. In the eighth issue of the *Conseiller*, Niboyet proposed a plan to set up four schools for poor children, two for boys and two for girls (from the age of seven until twelve). A few months later she devoted a long article to the day care centers of Lyon. [31] There the children of the poor were instructed in reading, writing, arithmetic, as well as in physical activities and religious training. They were taught how to use soap and water and how to eat proper food. In short they were taught how to manage their lives.

All of these projects: the schools for poor children, the day care centers, and the Athenée, required the support of the Lyonese women, especially of bourgeois women who had money to spare. Niboyet pointed out the need for the combined efforts of all women to help fund these projects. [32]

She, along with Louise Maignaud, believed that one day soon there would be a big step forward in the world, and that then it would become clear to all that women must be treated equally. But the effort in speeding the coming of that day should be made mostly by women. They were the interested party. They must support their own rights; their cause was too just for it not to triumph. "In the near future, many prejudices must fall before a peaceful coalition as in other days the feudal towers of the Bastille fell in front of an armed people for the conquest of their rights." [33] In short, Niboyet and Maignaud thought that the nineteenth century would be called the century of women, that in every part of Europe the most enlightened men seemed to have taken upon themselves the task of lifting the condition of women. [34]

But despite this show of optimism, the *Conseiller des Femmes* ceased to appear in September 1834, only eleven months after its first issue. We have no explanation for this fact. The following month, Eugenie Niboyet addressed the subscribers to the *Conseiller* in an editorial in the *Mosaique Lyonnaise* in which she said that the *Conseiller* would no longer appear and that subscribers would now receive the *Mosaique* in lieu of the *Conseiller*. [35] The *Mosaique* kept Eugenie as associate editor, and Leon Boitel as editor and publisher.

The *Mosaique* tried to broaden its readership by changing focus from feminist issues to literature, mostly written by women. Many of the authors from the *Conseiller* began to contribute to the *Mosaique*-- Elisabeth Celnart, Louise Maignaud, and of course Niboyet. The *Mosaique* also introduced two male poets, François Durand and Florvil; in spite of the change in format, the *Mosaique* was not successful either. It ceased publication after four months (January 18, 1835, was the last issue).

Like the feminists, several socialist thinkers challenged the traditional view of women; Cabet's pamphlet, *La Femme* published in 1848 is illustrative of the problems faced by socialists when confronted with "the woman question." The contents of this pamphlet: "her special qualities, her rights, her unhappy position in society, the cause of her unhappiness and its remedy in the community" [36] were indicative of a melange of old ideas about women applied to the new realities of the industrial age. For Cabet, woman was naturally graceful and beautiful; but industrial society placed the majority of women, the women of the proletariat (he did not call the women proletarians) in a desperate situation.

Cabet dramatically described the life of these women, born in misery, on piles of straw, who received nothing from their fathers but polluted blood and from their mothers, insufficient milk. [37] From their first steps in the muck of their homes they got used to a lifetime of filth and rags. As children, they were burdened with excessive and repulsive work in unhealthy conditions which destroyed the freshness of their youth. As they grew older, Cabet continued, their extreme poverty deprived many of them of the opportunity of being wives and mothers and condemned them to the inconveniences and dangers of momentary attachments which were greatly facilitated by the close working quarters of men and women. [38] As for married women, they were often tortured by frustrated, brutal, drunk, lazy, or sick husbands. The "women of the proletariat" worked while pregnant, while nursing, and even in old age.

Cabet's awareness of the plight of most women led him to refute the feminist position that all women, workers and bourgeoisie, were sisters. He recognized that the significant distinction was not between men and women, but rather between rich people and poor people. The real cause of the suffering of the "women of the proletariat" was not that they were women, but that society supported a poor majority and an opulent minority. [39] This was partly true, but even Cabet failed to recognize the significant link between the employment of women and the exploitation of the working class. Despite his trips to Lyon, he failed to see the "women of the proletariat" as women workers who were employed in increasing numbers at very low wages.

Cabet's solution to the problems faced by working women is illustrative of his failure to grasp the real cause of their dilemma. Abstractly, Cabet advocated the equality of the sexes. But, practically he said that the family was to be retained as the basic unit of society, and the father recognized as its head. [40] To eliminate the problems caused by bad husbands, he assured that in his community there would be no brutal, lazy or sick men or women. Instead, "Man, taking Reason and Nature for his guides, would put his happiness in woman and making her

47

almost his idol, would spend his time making her happy.''[41] In theory, woman was placed on a pedestal, but, practically, she would spend her time being a good daughter, a good sister, a good wife, a good mother, and a good housekeeper.[42] Cabet's pamphlet illustrated the dichotomy of views on the subject of women in the 1840's: on the one hand she was an idol, on the other hand she existed only to help others.

This confusing image appealed to many Lyonese women workers who spoke hopefully about the day when they would enjoy happy lives in a Cabetist community. Flora Tristan, a socialist-feminist who visited Lyon in 1843 and '44, complained about the naivete of these women who believed in Cabet's schemes.[43] Tristan had her own plan which she addressed to all workers--men and women--in a pamphlet called, *L'Union Ouvrière*. She believed that the worker's family life was a significant cause of the degraded position of women in society.

Tristan built her case by describing the personal history of working women. As young children, she reported, they were left in the care of their uneducated mothers and grandmothers, some of whom were brutal and beat their daughters for no reason, others who were weak and careless and let their daughters do whatever they wanted. Many vacillated from one extreme to the other so that the girls were brought up with wild contradictions.[44] The latter conditions reflected Tristan's own childhood spent with an uneducated and frustrated mother.

Tristan continued her presentation of the life of women workers by explaining that young boys were often sent to school, while the girls usually stayed home to work--cleaning house, taking care of younger siblings, cooking and shopping. Having herself received no formal education, she was sensitive to the fact that by the age of 12 most girls were apprenticed to craftsmen who exploited them by using them as domestic help, rather than teaching them a skill. Beatings were frequent, and the continual injustice and brutality left emotional scars. Many girls became hard, unjust, wicked women by the age of 20.[45]

Often, these women married without affection, merely to escape their parents. Their husbands, more educated, legally the head of the household, and paid twice the wages of women, treated their wives with disdain. Recalling the early days of her own marriage, Tristan explained that the polarization between superior husband and inferior wife resulted in many scenes of violence, and an atmosphere of constant irritation. The husband, seeking an outlet from his tiny flat charged with tensions, sought refuge in the cabaret.[46] Tristan explained that the working husband had no place else to go since most of them no longer believed in the church, nor did they understand the theater, nor were they permitted to meet with groups of workers. Wives who counted on their husbands' wages were discouraged to see how much went to the cabaret.

The woman worker's life history soon included children and that meant several new mouths to feed. Four or five crying children added to the tense atmosphere of the small apartments. Children saw their father infrequently, and when they did, he was usually irritable or drunk. Their mother complained about him all the time, and the children often hated their father as a result. They feared their mother; they obeyed her, but they did not love her either; Tristan had obeyed her own mother by marrying her first employer, a lithographer named André Chazal. And then, the cycle repeated itself.

In sum, Tristan emphasized, working women were not taught how to manage their households, nor how to raise children; they were equally ignorant of good housekeeping and the essentials of hygiene. And, unlike their bourgeois counterparts, they were unable to afford the luxuries of hiring a housekeeper and a governess to manage for them. Tristan insisted that working women were not naturally brutal, but became so as a result of their harshness of their life experiences. She urged working men, in their own self-interest, to improve their family life by correcting this situation. The first thing they must do according to Tristan was to extend the Declaration of the Rights of Man issued in 1789 to a Declaration of the Rights of Men and Women.[47]

Far more significant than this symbolic gesture was her suggestion that an equal number of boys and girls be admitted into the first Workers' Palace, a center for study, recreation, and nursing for young and old.[48] Her plan called for the children to enter at the age of six. They would receive basic hygiene and grooming instructions, would eat good food, and get sufficient exercise, and wear simple, useful uniforms, without corsets for the girls nor ties for the boys.[49] Each child would choose a craft, but would be obliged to perfect an alternative craft before leaving the Palace. From the age of ten, each child would receive part of the money he earned from his work. This part would increase each year until he reached 18 and graduated.

Tristan's plan specified that boys and girls should receive equal pay for equal work. She reasoned that equal pay for equal work was not only just, but it was a necessity for the working class, for without it employers would soon hire only women to do equal work at less pay (as occurred in Lyon) and eventually discover ways to employ only children at even less pay. [50] Thus, Tristan's sympathy for the plight of women workers led her to the important conclusion that paying women half-wages was not only unjust to the women involved, but in the long run it jeopardized the jobs of all the men.

Though, like the feminists of the *Conseiller,* Tristan began with the idea that management and order were crucial for workers' households, her investigation led her to the then radical demand of equal pay. But, let us not forget, one of the primary purposes of this demand was to keep jobs open for men so that they could support their wives and small children. Despite the radical flavor of the rhetoric from each of the media discussed above: "sisterhood" from the feminists," "sexual equality" from Cabet, and "equal pay" from Tristan, their overriding impact was to encourage women not to upset their role in the family. These media reinforced the belief of S. Hugont, a mechanic from Lyon who wrote in 1844:

> *Women should have a quiet life, good to raise children in, tranquility in which to give children their first education. Man has always been a savage, while women always consecrated themselves to the interior life. I don't mean that she should obey as a slave does his master, but I don't think the social order should be disturbed.* [51]

They were buttressed further by the influence of the church and the school.

Chapter IV

THE CHURCH: SALVATION AND INDUSTRIAL TRAINING

The silk workers of Lyon were sharply divided in their feelings about the Catholic Church. The anti-clericalism of master weavers, largely a function of their opposition to convent-workshop competition, became a cultural attitude which tended to alienate them from women workers who remained loyal to the Church for practical and spiritual reasons. This cleavage of opinion divided families, neighborhoods, and had a profound effect on the emerging working class still sub-divided by craft traditions, geographic origins and skill-level.

In his memoires, Norbert Truquin, a Lyonese silk weaver, recalled the tenacity of religious customs. He described his intention to have a civil marriage ceremony (in the late 1850's) and the pressure put on him by his friends who urged him to have a church ceremony in order not to go against the wishes of his fiancée and her family (all silk workers). "[My friends] argued that I had to fight to overcome my personal repugnance for the church . . . they indoctrinated me so well that instead of following my own ideas, I agreed to their wishes."[1]

Truquin was destined to meet with much more religious sentiment amongst the people. Soon after he married he moved into a flat opposite the Convent of Saint-Joseph in the Croix-Rousse. One morning he observed about 2,000 women gathered in the courtyard of the convent. He asked his neighbor, a sixty-year old widow and his reeler, what was the cause of the gathering. "They belong to the Compagnie de Jesus as I do," she replied. After having explained that there were several branches and that she belonged to a different one, she went on to state the reason for their meeting: "Those you see here have come to get the *mot d'ordre* and the vouchers for bread and coal." Truquin asked what the former was but was dissatisfied with the elusive response that was forthcoming: "What they have to do next."[2]

Truqin tried to get to the root of this woman's affiliation with the church. He asked her how she could belong to the Compagnie de Jesus when her husband had been a republican, a follower of Raspail. Did she negate her husband's ideas? The widow (of five years) answered that she was old and poor and that in going to church she found a distraction. Further, when she fell sick the church helped her out a little, whereas "from the republicans one never gets anything but misery and contempt for riches."[3]

Truquin discovered how deep were the widow's convictions when he fell sick and spent several days in bed. After he recuperated the widow came to see him and they had the following interchange:

> *Why haven't you come to see me for the past few days?*
>
> *I thought that you weren't going to get well and I was waiting for the last moment to bring you a priest.*
>
> *You mean you were waiting until I didn't have enough strength to protest?*
>
> *Yes.*
>
> *But you know that I don't believe in that. . . .*[4]

The widow's belief in the church and her efforts to extend her faith to others in her class were not unique. Truquin reported that some women went to the extent of having their husbands arrested for having led them astray with their opinions against the church. These women reported that they preferred the church which helped them to live and raise their families to their own husbands. Truquin believed that there were many women like that amongst the working poor. Almost all of the concierge's wives were affiliated with the Société de Jésus in his estimation.[5]

On the other hand, amongst master weavers there was a long tradition of protest against the church. As early as 1769, a silk weaver and the father of eight children, Bocen, protested the frequent holy observances:

> I see the coming of holy days with fright. I confess to you that I barely abstain from cursing them. . . . Wouldn't Sunday be enough? Wouldn't it be better celebrated if it were unique? . . . We are up to the third holy day of Christmas week: I've pawned my furniture; I've secured a week's advance from my bourgeois; I'm short on bread. How will I get by the fourth holy day? That's not all: there are four more holy days next week. Good heavens! Eight holy days in a fortnight. 6

Bocen the silk weaver was not opposed to the church; he was critical specifically of monks and monasteries and the numerous holy days. He further blamed "the rich" for encouraging these celebrations in order to reap profit from their cabarets and brothels which did big business on holy days. 7 The identity of interests between the rich and the church in contrast to the often preached special concern of the church for the humble proved a continuous source of frustration throughout the nineteenth century.

In 1844, Proudhon on a visit to Lyon provided us with an early description of this phenomenon: "When the elite of society go in one direction, the people go in the other; since the powerful (of Lyon) have turned to the church, the people have abandoned it." He described the "multitude" of Lyonese families where all ties with the church had been broken: Children were no longer baptized; church weddings were no longer performed; first communions were abandoned; religious burials neglected. 8

Anti-clerical sentiment strengthened during 1848. The Capucins and the Jesuits were expelled; public schools were instituted to replace Catholic schools in the Croix-Rousse and La Guillotiere worker suburbs. The number of civil marriages and burials increased. By 1850, the Procureur General of Lyon defined socialism in his city as a sort of fanatic faith built on the ruins of religious sentiment. 9

Two years later, Boniface de Vaise was arrested for creating an anti-Catholic religion. He baptized the children of socialist parents with the following incantation: "Child, I baptise you in the name of the democratic and social republic, of liberty, equality and fraternity.[10] These "baptised" children were obliged never to enter a church and automatically became members of the Carbonari society.

In 1856 when Louis Reybaud investigated Lyonese workers he found them completely detached from Catholicism. The weavers whom he interviewed explained that they were scientific positivists.[11] Audiganne found similar evidence. He concluded that religious habits had lost even more ground than family ties amongst the workers. Even those workers who still followed their religion adhered to the rituals without any inner conviction. When there was fear of catastrophe, like flood or epidemic, Audiganne found a speedy revival of religious sentiment; but this reawakening was shortlived and often superstitious. He concluded that most people stayed away from the clergy for fear that they would be encouraged to bear their burdens more docilely.[12]

The increasing dissatisfaction with monks, holy days, and the clergy developed into an election issue in 1859. The workers who voted for Prud'hommes elected only those candidates who had no trace of religious sentiments.[13] Gradually the Procureur General began to fear that this anti-clerical feeling would coalesce into an anti-religious worker movement.[14] These fears gained ground in 1867 when the first violently anti-clerical weekly, *Le Reveil,* appeared. It was followed in rapid succession by *Le Refusé, L'Avant-Garde,* and *L'Excommunié,* weeklies which had record circulation for provincial journals of this period, selling about 5 to 6,000 copies.[15]

In the 1860's the term *"parti clerical"* became synonymous with enemy of the people. For example, when the price of bread went up the workers blamed it on the clerical party. Likewise when there was unemployment priests were blamed with fomenting agitation and paralyzing work. Workers complained even when the church dispensed aid to the unemployed, demanding work, not charity. They accused the clergy of being bigots by distributing aid only to those who attended church.[16]

Anti-clerical views did not reflect the majority opinion of the Lyonese working class. While anti-clericalism was highly developed among artisan weavers of the Croix-Rousse and socialist leaders of La Guillotière, it was not widespread among the mass of workers coming in from the countryside and certainly not among women workers.[17] The church did not ignore the repeated challenges from artisan workers and tried vigorously to win back the affection of her waning flock by adopting a new plan.

In a sermon delivered by Abbé Bez, curé of the parish of Oullins (near Lyon), on February 12, 1836, the strategy of the Catholic Church was revealed. In the industrializing world of nineteenth century France, the Church would become industrial:

> *The Church takes the centuries as she finds them . . . in our day she will become industrial, but she will make this industry Christian; she will not permit the bubbling activity of this century to be solely occupied in search of material goods which must escape it sooner or later, but she will fix her attention on a more solid and more durable good, the treasures of the after-life.* [18]

Thus Abbé Bez unfolded the new banner of the Church: socialization of the faithful for the industrializing world, while not neglecting their souls. Bez went on to specify the tactics essential to this new strategy:

> *A new era has commenced for this Holy Religion, and if she no longer builds magnificent houses of prayer and contemplation uniquely concerned with heavenly promises, she raises with zeal numerous workshops, where she congregates men very thirsty to do good, to aid by their counsel the young generations who are perverse to becoming better.* [19]

To insure the success of the dual program--salvation and industrial training--Abbé Bez and many other priests believed that it was essential to set up workshops within convents and monasteries, which they called *providences*. Nowhere was this plan more thoroughly developed than in Lyon.

To convince the leading silk magnates to support the industrialization of convents and monasteries, that is to provide capital for machinery and in some cases new buildings, the clergy brought forth the traditional argument about human nature:

> *If misery were the sole cause of crime, then it would be sufficient to give them [the poor] bread or the means of earning it honestly to detach them from their criminal habits; but most often vice has more profound roots. . .*[20]

If mankind was plagued with profound vice, the Church had experience in curing it. Bez continued, "To enchain the passions, to rectify the judgment of the unhappy plunged into such mistakes, to revive in them the sentiment of the dignity of man and his duty to God . . . one needs a strong force like Christian charity."[21]

The Abbé emphasized that the Church alone was capable of calling to her the impoverished inhabitants of the countryside, and of initiating them into the secrets of the silk industry: then the new recruits would become skillful masters and in their turn teach others who were uprooted from corruption and laziness by the Church. And what would their reward be? "A little bread to feed them, the promise to die peacefully in the home you have opened for them and finally, the hope of being happy for eternity."[22]

In return for a small investment, the Church was offering to provide the inner compulsion so necessary to the transformation of a pre-industrial people to an industrial one. Bez explained that it would be impossible to arrive at the "best results for the happiness of society" without the powerful help of religion. By the unique influence of the promises it held out only the Church would be able to break the will of the most rebellious and enflame their hearts to perfect devotion.

With the coming of industrialism little was heard of the old incentives to labor which had existed in artisan society--family and community responsibilities, joy in craftsmanship. Work was now frankly regarded as an imposition which only a strong constitution could bear, preferably one fortified by the Church. The early monastic founders had various motives for including labor as part of their regime, but their most characteristic attitude was to regard work as a mortification of the flesh, a remedy for idleness, not a productive good in itself. [23] In nineteenth century monasteries, however, the positive merit of hard work was as clearly asserted for Catholics as it had been for Protestants during the Reformation.

It was with the new goal of industrial training that the clergy turned their attention to the poor. Claudine Thévènet, founder of the *providence* at Fourvière, described the commencement of the socialization process: young girls who had been removed from their family farms or workshops at the age of 10 came in disheveled and "disgusting" and were immediately scrubbed and deloused. Their clothing was replaced by clean dress and they were given shoes. They were required to sign contracts of apprenticeship which stressed the virtues of obedience, submission to the sisters who were charged with regulating the girls' demeanor and instruction, and adherence to all regulations at the convent. Attendance was strictly required; no time was allowed for the girls to visit with their families without the permission of the director. [24]

A contract of apprenticeship to a convent-workshop discovered by Reybaud in the 1850's included the following conditions of apprenticeship:

1. *Only girls between 13 and 15 years of age, of good morality and good health, who can present a vaccination certificate will be accepted.*
2. *The girl will be paid, fed and lodged.*
3. *The student vouches obedience, submission to the forewomen charged with her demeanor and instruction.*
4. *Only the director has the right to authorize or deny exits; these grants will be made only at the request of the father of the girl.*

Girls would be stimulated to produce by paying them 40-50 francs the first year, 60-75 francs the second year, and 80-100 francs the third year, for a twelve-hour workday. Their remuneration depended on "overall behavior, the quantity and quality of work, submissiveness and diligence." Any apprentice sent home due to bad behavior would forfeit her wages for the year, and her father would be charged 100 francs by the *providence* as damages for not fulfilling the contract. [25]

The liberal bourgeois reformers supported these convent-workshops. They saw these cloisters as an excellent opportunity to help the masses. Jane Dubuisson expressed their view: "A large number of children remain, because of their parents' neglect, left to their bad inclinations. It is from this mass of abandoned children who expose their misery and degradation on the public squares that emerge the unhappy ones who begin by being ignorant and lazy and finish up in crime and then go on to expiate their faulty education in prison." [26]

The master craftsmen, however, saw the convent-workshops in a very different light. They were predisposed to suspect collusion between the rich and the church and now focused on the unfair competition that the convent-workshop became for the family workshop. Stories about overwork and poor diet as well as complaints about sexual perversion within the *providences* fueled the growing unrest. Weavers who continued to lose their shops, their looms and even their professions during the 1840's frequently singled out the convent-workshop, supported by the church and the silk tycoons as their special enemy. They complained that establishments in which laborers worked and lived together were unfair competition to the individual weaver. Some demanded the right for workers to organize into large cooperative workshops of their own, which were illegal, to be able to compete with the low prices of the convents. Others urged that a special tax be imposed on convents which manufactured silk and that the proceeds of that tax be used to aid needy workers.

The consensus of worker opinion was that the convents, ostensibly religious communities which established workshops to provide employment and thus help the poor, actually hurt them by exploiting young women of worker families and competing unfairly with the master weavers. Unlike the testimony left by the clergy, the evidence from the worker press and from police reports corroborates this allegation.

For example, there was a 'philanthropic-mercantile-religious' institution near Lyon which received poor young girls under the age of 21 in order to teach them a skill. M. David, a mechanic who lived at Rey 7, in the Croix-Rousse, brought his daughter, Louise Françoise, there in 1842 when she was twelve years old. She was brought home to him five years later in a state of infirmity which made her permanently incapable of earning a living. Duviard, the physician who examined

Louise, confirmed that she had incurable deformities which seemed to be the result of forced work, too difficult for the girl, coupled with insufficient care, poor hygiene, and living for a prolonged period in a very damp place.[27]

Forced and premature work under unhealthy conditions were not the only problems in these workshops. In the Croix-Rousse, on Marnobles St., there was an establishment for young girls seemingly founded by the Church, specifically devoted to making silk and silk garments.[28] The establishment held 35-40 girls, ranging in age from 11 to 20, who received no other instruction than that associated with the skills of their trade. The girls were housed in dormitories. During the night, an unknown 'demon', perhaps several, entered their rooms and frightened them. The noisy demon did not restrict himself to loud menacing sounds, he shook their beds, took off the blankets and "did not always stop with the wickedness of an immaterial spirit." The girls cried and pleaded, but the demon explained that he was there to correct their faults. Their teacher severely criticized their attempts to stop the demon, who she explained, came to punish them for their sins.

In July 1847, during the absence of the headmistress, a devil announced himself to two girls sharing a bed. He declared that he came in the name of the grand master to exercise his power on this institute. One of the girls said that she was not afraid and was rewarded for her bravery with being beaten on her ears and nose and then having the skin on her arms and thighs torn by a metal tweezer.

This institute was run by Mlle. Denis and her brother. After an investigation, Mlle. Denis was forced to close her institute and to pay a modest fine of five francs for having run it without a license. The girls who still had homes to return to were sent home. The others were transferred to other institutions. Though Cardinal de Bonald protested vehemently that this establishment was not affiliated in any way with the Church,[29] many workers refused to believe that the Church and the rich were not acting in cahoots here as in many other religious-mercantile institutions.

Since these establishments came under increasing attack by workers in the 1840's, some monasteries employed the system of kidnapping and imprisoning their young workers. Police reports from Lyon in August

1847 disclosed the kidnapping procedure. [30] Dungeons were discovered in several convents in the area. Cries of girls being held involuntarily by the Convent of Bethlehem, the Ladies of Calvaire, the Ladies of St. Elizabeth and the Ladies of Marie Thérèse were heard in the streets. These convents used strait jackets to punish their girls; they shaved their heads and imprisoned them in dungeons.

During an investigation conducted in September 1847, Françoise Faure, 22 years old, told the court that she was brought to a convent at the request of her parents. Mlle. Faure did not wish to leave the convent, but she did want to see her mother. The sisters would not allow her mother to visit. Mlle. Faure described how she was placed in the dungeon three times, held fast by a strait jacket, because she refused to do any more work. The first time she was held in the dungeon for three days and nights. The second time they left her there for thirteen days and nights, and the last time for four days and nights. When she was released her hands and arms were swollen because the restraints had been pulled too tight. As a result she was not able to work for several days. [31]

Convents which housed 80-100 girls, some brought in forcibly, others ensnared by false descriptions of their duties, were not uncommon. Dungeons, chains, and strait jackets were part of the equipment in these establishments. Drugs were also used to 'tranquilize' the youngsters. Once inside, the 'captives' were not permitted to communicate freely with their family or friends nor with each other. Parents were very seldom allowed to visit their children and when a visit was permitted a nun or monk was present at all times to monitor the questions and dictate the responses. [32]

A letter in the weaver's press, *L'Echo de la Fabrique,* of July 31, 1844, summarized the growing worker opposition to the convent-workshops:

> *Run through the laughing hills which surround our city, and you will see these industrial prisons rising on all sides, proud and arrogant. Here is the Sainte-Famille, a little further on is the Providence, there is the Sacré-Coeur, the Solitude.... There are the establishments where the most sordid interests are hidden under a cloak of sacredness and of religion and charity; the*

establishments in which the founders speculate on the work and the nourishment of the young whom they exploit in order to triple their capital. These establishments which work and live in common, create an unbearable competition for the master craftsman who cannot support his family while working for the same price. 33

The workers were opposed to the hypocrisy of the church which exploited young workers' children in the name of charity; they were further enraged at the price-cutting engaged in by the convent-workshops.

On May 20, 1847, the silk workers of Lyon presented a petition to the Chamber of Deputies in Paris demanding that all workshops within religious communities be closed down.

We the undersigned, silk workers in the city of Lyon, have the honor to submit to you, with respect, a fact of public notoriety to wit: most religious establishments in out department and in surrounding departments manufacture silk cloth, especially unpatterned silk cloth; that in several of these establishments attempts are being made for the manufacture of lace; and that if things continue this way it is likely that in a number of years the cloisters will turn into real workshops against whose wealth and power we the poor workers cannot fight in any way. 34

The petition went on to describe how the workers had been misled by the Cardinal de Bonald, the chief religious leader of Lyon. When the Cardinal assumed his office in 1840 he had promised that he would shortly put an end to the workshops within the religious communities because he understood that the working population of Lyon might be "inconvenienced" by them in time. For seven years they had waited and far from disestablishing workshops, the work in religious communities had grown significantly.

Political leaders in Paris began to take interest in the matter when the Parisian workers' newspaper, *La Democratie Pacifique* advocated a change in tactics. Workers should cease demanding the closing down of convent-workshops and begin demanding the freedom to live and work in common in their own associations. The Procureur General was concerned that the religious houses had demonstrated to the workers the desirability of organizing their work within phalansteries or other types of communes. [35]

Cardinal de Bonald answered the protests by denying that there were sufficient numbers of young people reeling in the *providences* of Lyon to provide serious competition for the family workshops. He estimated the total number of girls and women weaving in the convents at 500. [36] But this number is probably inaccurate. Abbé Bez (in 1840) estimated as follows: St-Bruno - 60 girls; St-Louise - 60 girls; Sacre-Coeur - 80 girls; Providence de Mlle Desmarets at Chaunette - 45 girls and at Passage - 60 girls; Les St-Michel - more than 200 girls. The total came to 505, but did not include the girls who worked at the Providence de la rue Scala, which he described as very flourishing, or those at Providence des Jeunes Economes. Neither mentions the providence at Fourvière. [37]

Even these figures inadequately describe the impact of the convent-workshops on the employment situation in Lyon. Abbé Bez explained that the merchants of Lyon preferred to purchase cloth from the convent-workshops because they appreciated the integrity of the *providence* and felt assured of getting their material on time and having top quality. [38] Thus, even when most of the workers of the city were unemployed, the religious workshops had orders to complete. Claudine Thévènet corroborated this statement by explaining that in the convents they did not follow the strikes of the workers. If the merchants gave them orders, they filled them regardless of whether or not the silk workers were striking. [39]

The hostility of the workers erupted on February 29, 1848, when news of the Parisian revolt reached Lyon. Dutacq described the destruction of the *providences* of Lyon and the surrounding communities of St- Genis, St-Etienne, Caluire, Sainte-Foy-les-Lyon, and Vaise by armed bands of workers. [40] The convent-workshops which escaped destruction were all temporarily closed down as were many of the religious primary schools.

But as soon as the heady atmosphere of the spring revolution passed, many of the convent-workshops reopened. Several demanded indemnities from the city government or the Department of the Rhône for the looms and other valuables they lost. [41] Cardinal de Bonald, despite the outbreak of violence directed at the Church's attempt at industrializing, continued to issue annual messages on this theme. In a message of 1853, he reiterated the idea first expressed by Abbé Bez in 1836, "The Church must regulate and sanctify industry." [42]

The Cardinal urged the industrialists to attain the well-being of mankind by making an alliance with the Catholic Church. He criticized the rapacious competition between businessmen and their willingness to sacrifice anything to their lust for lucre--which led to the increasing secularization of society by greedy employers who forced their employees to work on Sunday and holy days. The workers, De Bonald feared, no longer could distinguish between holy and workdays. "Losing belief in revealed truths," De Bonald predicted, "they'll finish by regarding them as fables with which to amuse children." [43]

De Bonald correctly predicted the secularization of the workers, though he was unaware of the role of the convent-workshop in that very process. Specifically, the *providences* forced their young workers to change from task-oriented work to time-oriented work. The former was work which was not cut-off from the rest of life, but was integrated into daily patterns of existence along with food preparation, child care, and religious rituals. This was the work pattern familiar to those brought up in artisan workshops or peasant farms. The latter was work which was segregated from all other aspects of life, but was related to the clock or the bell. In the *providence* workers did not see their family, nor talk to their friends. They learned that time was a currency, something to be used well. [44]

Though they declined in significance after mid-century, as they were replaced by factories, several convent-workshops continued to thrive through the turn of the century, switching from silk-making to dressmaking as their major product. In 1900 at least seven *providences* in Lyon housed 268 girls; in 1926, ten *providences* in the city and the surrounding countryside accommodated 400 to 500 girls; and, in 1976, three *providences* were still functioning in Lyon. [45]

Their longevity was due to the fact that they fulfilled several important functions. First, they provided a new role for the clergy who had to become more concerned with life on earth rather than in heaven in order to maintain their flock. Second, they enabled businessmen to produce more cheaply and therefore to amass more capital with which to promote further industrialization. Finally, they provided a chance for some workers mostly girls and some boys from rural backgrounds to make the transition from a pre-industrial outlook to an industrial one, while alienating the artisan elite.

Young girls taken into the cloisters were taught one additional lesson: women's work outside of the home is temporary. They were encouraged to fulfill their contracts of apprenticeship and then to return to the outside world, to marry and raise families. Even in the *providence,* where the time-discipline of women workers was perfected, women's jobs were still regarded as temporary employment. Religious and municipal schools reinforced this position. They too urged their girl pupils to be diligent, prompt and clean while in school or on the job; but women's real function, they concurred, was at home with the family.

Chapter V

CÉCILE AND JULIE: LEARNING TO BE A GOOD WOMAN

Girls who enrolled in primary schools in Lyon were taught almost exclusively by nuns, who needed no formal teaching certificate.[1] A "letter of obedience" from their superiors sufficed to qualify them. Most of the public schools set up as a result of the Loi Guizot (1833) endorsed the custom of entrusting primary school teaching to religious orders. In 1819 the Brothers of the Christian Doctrine were given 25,000 francs to fund their schools for working class boys, and in 1828 the Sisters of Saint Charles were awarded 3,000 francs to help defray their expenses in setting up a girls' school. In general the municipal government was called on to provide a schoolhouse and some furnishings--a teacher's desk, benches and tables, a clock, a crucifix, a map of France, and a portrait of the reigning monarch,[2] while the church provided the teachers.

By employing religious orders to teach primary schools, the bourgeoisie of the nineteenth century thwarted the educational goals of the Revolution. Condorcet's project for a national system of education (1792) argued that free education for every citizen would be:

> a way not only to assure to the nation more citizens able to serve and to the sciences more men capable of contributing to their progress, but also to diminish that inequality born of the difference of fortunes and to unite the classes that difference tends to separate.[3]

But, in the post-revolutionary period, the goal of uniting the classes through education was dropped. Substituted in its place was Guizot's philosophy of education:

> *Primary education has a vital role in preserving order and social stability and forming good citizens; faith in Providence, the sacredness of duty, submission to paternal authority, and the respect due to law, to the ruler and to the rights of all, such are the sentiments which (the teacher) will endeavor to develop.* [4]

Following the revolution of 1848, the church was called on to save society. Faced with the choice, in Montalembert's words, between socialism and catechism, [5] the bourgeoisie chose the latter. The priests had convinced the bourgeoisie that they were the friend of property and order and the next major education law--the Loi Falloux of 1850--reinforced the hegemony of the religious orders over primary education for the poor. [6]

Religious schools would maintain the established order, Bishop Dupanloup of Orleans wrote, "education must accommodate itself to the social and providential position of the pupil, to the role which he is called on to fill in society." [7] Far from abetting social mobility, or even sanctioning the rights of all, education was to reinforce social positions sanctified by Providence, hence unchangeable. The ultramontane Abbé Gouget worked out the details of this view. Education, he urged, should be kept within wise limits for too much education resulted in social calamity. Primary education should therefore be limited to prayer, reading and writing. Three-quarters of the students should not read well enough to enjoy it because they would only read corrupting literature or study the civil code and bring up too many petty cases for litigation. [8]

Liberals and conservatives concurred that moral and religious education should be put at the top of the list of primary school subjects. [9] But though they agreed that religious teaching should be the foundation of the education of the people, [10] the principle was not equally applied to girls and boys. Catholic education was seen as particularly suitable to girls since it stressed obedience and discipline, qualities believed to be a natural part of the female sphere, while independent thought seemed to be more appropriate for the "stronger sex." Middle class parents

66

sent their daughters to private religious schools and their sons to schools which emphasized science and skills. Working class parents had less choice but displayed similar tendencies. Some of their boys went to secular public schools and some had the option of attending secondary schools which were skill-oriented. The daughters of the working class, on the other hand, were taught almost exclusively by religious orders. Of the 256 communes in the Rhône Valley all but 18 had a school for girls by 1836--85 of them were run by the Sisters of St-Joseph, 56 by the Sisters of St- Charles. [11] The chart below shows the distribution of 12,514 students in primary schools in Lyon and its suburbs in 1844: [12]   (See page 68.)

Regular school attendance was quite different from the traditional experience of artisanal life where work and play took place in the home for the entire family. The idea of childhood and education as a distinct phase of life preceding entry into the work world did not correspond to the *canut*'s life in the workshop where boys and girls were expected to do their share as soon as they were able. Thus the concept of full-time schooling had to be imposed by the authorities. Since primary education did not become compulsory until 1879, the municipal authorities had to convince parents that it was a worthwhile sacrifice of income to send their children to school. In Lyon this was achieved by a combination of carrot and stick methods.

The lure was the promise of a better life and upward social mobility for the children. In a broadside titled, "Reopening of Schools," the mayor of the Croix-Rousse urged parents to send their children to school because instruction was so necessary in all positions of life, so useful in forming character and developing the intellect that it was offered free to those who could not pay. The mayor hoped that the importance of this benefit would be recognized by the parents and that they would fulfill their parental duties by sending their children to school. Without any sacrifice on the part of working parents, they could contribute to the prosperity of their own families and the well-being of the nation. [13] Periodic money awards to *canut* school children reinforced this message. Thus when the Duke of Orleans visited Lyon in 1839 bankbooks with deposits of 50 francs were awarded to the best students. [14]

	Religious Orders	Mutual (Secular)	Lamartinière (Secular)	Protestant	Jewish	Total
Lyon: Boys	3,394	691	290	90	30	4,205
Lyon: Girls	3,466	527	—	102	—	4,095
Croix-Rousse: Boys	803	90	—	—	—	893
Croix-Rousse: Girls	750	—	—	—	—	750
Guillotiere: Boys	1,220	—	—	—	—	1,220
Guillotiere: Girls	810	—	—	—	—	810
Vaise: Boys	301	—	—	—	—	301
Vaise: Girls	240	—	—	—	—	240

The stick was the threat that children who didn't go to school would wind up in trouble. The Abbé Desgorges explained that most children fell into a state of vagabondage as a result of the brutality and neglect of their parents.[15] There were sufficient examples of young women arrested for vagrancy or prostitution and young men for theft or violent crimes for parents to heed the repeated warnings of priests and government officials to send their children to school.

Thus more and more working class girls were sent to school with the promise of brighter futures if they attended classes regularly. These promises for upward mobility as we have already seen were the silver lining in the bourgeois cloud of fear of the workers and the desire of municipal and business leaders to keep these girls in their place both as women and as workers. Years later Emile Durkheim formulated this educational dilemma:

> *Society can only function if there exists among its members a unity of purpose and outlook. Education perpetuates and reinforces that unity by imprinting upon the mind of the child the essential values upon which collective life rests. However, on the other hand, total cooperation in society would be impossible without a certain diversity. Education itself assures the persistence of that diversity through progressive specialization. Looked at from either aspect, education consists of the deliberate and methodological socialization of the younger generation.*[16]

The essential values of industrializing France--cleanliness, punctuality, order, hard work for future rewards--were imposed by teachers. A war on *patois* and imposition of the metric system in all the schools were designed to create national unity. At the same time, diversity of class roles was assured by the maintenance of private schools for the wealthy and public schools for the poor. In the list of 367 pupils run by Sisters of St. Charles (below) parents' occupations are all working class. Diversity of sex roles--specifically imposing woman's modern role definition--was a unique function of girls' primary education.

Occupations of Pupils' Parents

--Sisters of St. Charles School, 1836

276 silk workers

19 cabaret workers

12 day workers

10 shoemakers

8 tailors

7 gardeners

5 salesmen

5 masons

4 bakers

4 textile workers

4 carpenters

4 mechanics

3 butchers

3 laundresses

The new values and roles in society sought by the bourgeoisie were to be achieved by instilling habits of thought and action in the primary schools. Habits learned in childhood, not subject to reasoning, would produce a strong emotional appeal. [18] But to achieve this goal and to accommodate the increasing numbers of students, a new method of instruction had to be devised. The old system, or individual method, allowed each child to learn from his own books, often legal documents belonging to the family, while the teacher called up pupils one at a time to quiz them and to give them their next task. This system met the needs when there were very few pupils, no money for books, and no need to instill new values. An alternative, the mutual system, accommodated many pupils (sometimes 100-200) by employing the advanced pupils to work as monitors, directing groups of their peers. This sytem was too undisciplined from the viewpoint of the religious orders who devised their own method--the simultaneous sytem.[19]

In primary schools run by the religious orders, and increasingly in the secular primary schools of Lyon, the pupils were taught simultaneously, as a single unit, by a single instructor. The school was usually divided into three classes, corresponding to beginner, intermediate and advanced work. The new method made possible the use of oral exposition in teaching and work based on common books and exercises, also created by the religious orders. The simultaneous system encouraged automatic responses to predictable questions designed to insure the firm habits of thought and action described above. It was the spirit of the catechism adopted for classroom use in all subject areas.

The Regulations for Primary Schools of the Croix-Rousse, published in 1838, helps to focus our picture of the new classroom dynamics. The essential rules were:

1. *Students in each class must all have the same books.*
2. *No student can be promoted without having completed all the work in his present class.*
3. Patois *must be eliminated.*
4. *Report cards will be distributed monthly.*
5. *Names of the best pupils will be prominently displayed.*
6. *Daily lesson plans must be submitted by teachers.*
7. *Religious principles and duties must be constantly emphasized by the teacher.*
8. *Teacher will check pupils' cleanliness daily and require those who do not meet the standard to wash.*
9. *Absences and tardiness will be recorded and parents of repeated offenders will be called in.*

*10. Expulsion is to be used as a punishment; no
corporal punishment is permitted.* [20]

The rules emphasized uniformity of standards, hierarchy of classes,
religious duty, cleanliness and promptness; those who followed the
rules were rewarded by a system of delayed gratification, those who
failed to follow were removed from the system. The spirit of the new
method was revealed in the physical set-up of the school which was
designed to reinforce the values being taught in class. Unlike previous
generations of artisan and peasant children, the pupils attending school
in our period did not sit at desks facing each other. Rather the furniture
prescribed for primary schools from the 1830's were individual desks,
set in rows, all facing the teacher, who sat at a large desk, often on a
platform, in front of the classroom. Each pupil faced the teacher. [21] The
emphasis on doing your own work and rivalry among students now all
working out of the same books replaced the natural camaraderie of
children facing each other, working out of different books and therefore
not in a competitive situation.

In this setup, pupils were quick to imbibe the bourgeois meaning of
"liberty, equality and fraternity." In the class all the children seemed
to have an equal opportunity to succeed--they had the same books, the
same desks, took the same exams, but some pupils did well and others
failed. The students were taught that each got his just rewards. This
was superb training for life in nineteenth century France where
Guizot's answer to the clamoring poor was "enrichissez-vous." It was
important for bourgeois leaders to believe they merited their success. It
was even more important to them for workers to believe that they
merited their own failure. [22]

To reinforce the bourgeois ideas in the minds of students, uniform textbooks were introduced first by the religious orders and later in all
schools. One of the most popular for religious instruction was Fleury's
Catéchisme Historique which fit the needs of simultaneous instruction
with its text and its precise questions and answers. The following
excerpt is translated from the original as an example of the spirit of the
new education:

God made the world of nothing by his words and his will and for his glory. He did it in six days. The first day he created the heaven and the earth; then light; the second day he created the firmament which he called the sky; the third day he separated the water from the land, and made the earth bring forth the plants; on the fourth he made the sun, the moon and the stars; on the fifth he made the birds in the air and the fish in the sea; on the sixth he made animals on the earth and made man in his image; and God rested on the seventh day.

Questions: Who made the world?
Answer: God did.

Q: What did he made it out of?
A: Of nothing.

Q: How did he make it?
A: By his word.

Q: Why did he make it?
A: For his glory.

Q: In how many days did God create the world?
A: In six days.

Q: What did he make on the first day?
A: The heaven and the earth, later the light.

Q: And the second day?
A: The firmament which he called sky.

Q: What did he do on the third day?
A: He separated the water from the land and brought forth all sorts of plants.

Q: And the fourth day?
A: He created the sun, the moon, and the stars.

Q: And the fifth?
A: He made the birds in the air and the fish in the sea.

Q: And the sixth?
A:He made all the earth's animals and made man in His image.

Q: And on the seventh day?
A: After making all the things, he rested.

The text was presented; the questions were asked; the answers were given. Different questions, other answers had no room in the classrooms created by the Loi Guizot. This mentality was not limited to religious instruction, which authorities agreed was the main purpose of primary schools, but permeated all other areas as well.

Using the same method, Mme. Caillard wrote a collection of children's stories pursuing moral themes. The following is excerpted from "Jeanne or Bad Character": [24]

1. *Mr. and Mrs. Robert have only one little girl named Marie, who is about eight years old.*
2. *Marie has a cousin named Jeanne Perault who is about the same age.*
3. *Jeanne lives with her uncle Robert.*
4. *Poor thing! She has lost her mother and father.*
5. *She stayed with her grandparents for awhile, but they died too.*
6. *Marie was a good little girl; her mother taught her to obey.*
7. *There was a time when she carried on a bit, but that was when she was very young.*
8. *Her mother always made her leave the room when she cried, and never gave her what she asked for when she shouted....*
10. *Marie did what she was told; and soon after, ashamed of her reprimands, she returned saying: "Mother, I promise never to be bad again, forgive me, I beg of you."*

11. *Lucky Marie! You had a good mother! She took a lot of trouble to make you good-mannered! How much you must love her!*

12. *But, poor Jeanne had the bad luck of losing her mother.*

13. *Her grandmother did not know how to handle a young girl; to keep her from being bad. She let Jeanne do whatever she wanted.*

14. *And when Jeanne did not get what she wanted, she cried and tormented her grandmother.*

15. *Thus, not corrected, she became a bad little girl and was not happy.*

16. *Because a child who cries, who carries on, who is disobedient, cannot but be unhappy....*

26. *Marie is good and intelligent.*

27. *She is satisfied with what she has and doesn't always want what she can't have. That's why she is happy.*

28. *She is loved by all; if you knew her too little friends, I'm sure you would love her.*

29. *Jeanne, on the contrary, never tries to please anyone; she always finds fault with what others do and their happiness makes her sad.*

30. *She carries on at the slightest difficulty; that's why Jeanne isn't happy.*

32. *Remember that a violent nature brings our unhappiness and that of our parents.*

34. *And never forget, dear children, that sweetness will make us loved by all who know us.*

Caillard's story was followed by questions and answers directly based on the text. In this case the object was not historical "truth" but practical norms. Children were shown the misfortune that accrued to those who failed to internalize controls. Girls who studied this story knew that their roles as future mothers must encompass both love and discipline to mold children who wanted to be like their parents. [25]

If we turn to the pages of *La Recitation* by Louis Peigné, we see a similar method still being employed at the end of the century to further elaborate woman's mature role. [26] The stories in *La Recitation* effectively set up two spheres of activities: the female sphere which was bounded by the home; the male sphere which encompassed society at large. Men's world was described as very important requiring courage; woman's world was described as nurturant and loving, despite the fact that women were pictured as being weak, frail creatures.

The first story in the book, "Little Mother,"[27] illustrated both aspects of woman's character:

> *At night, when I am sleeping,*
> *Who comes to kiss me?*
> *Who smiles when I wake up?*
> *Little mother, it is you.*
>
> *Who reprimands tenderly?*
> *So tender, that when I hear it*
> *I repent immediately*
> *Little mother, it is you.*
>
> *Who is good and sweet to all?*
> *To the poor who are hungry and thirsty*
> *Who teaches men how to give?*
> *Little mother, it is you.*
>
> *When you grow old,*
> *It will be my turn to care for you,*
> *Who will return your tenderness?*
> *Little mother, I will.*

The moral of the story was clear: "The good mother must devote herself entirely to her children, who will thank her." This nurturant quality in mothers was not attributed to their learning skills, but rather to their natural female instincts "to mother." These feelings were further described in another popular children's book, *Mathilde et Gabrielle*. The author, Claire Guermante expressed the universality of the pleasures of maternity as well as the need to experience it in order to comprehend its joy. In a letter from the young mother Mathilde to her adopted sister, Gabrielle, Guermante elaborated:

*What delicious emotions in the thought: to be a mother
(it's the peak of happiness, heaven on earth); to hear
the first cry of her child, to nourish him with her milk, to
rock him in her arms, to see his first smile, receive
his first kiss and hear from his adorable mouth the
sweet name 'Mama'; all of these intimate joys cannot be
told, one must experience them to appreciate all of their
wonder. . . .*

The duties of a mother are sweet to fulfill. [28]

Though mothering was both natural and to be encouraged, in the view
of the textbooks, other qualities were to be discouraged. In *Le Moralist
du jeune age,* published in 1835, and reprinted in 1861 and 1863,
Antoine de St-Gervais presented an injunction against vanity by using
the metaphor of a rose. A young girl, Caroline, was in their garden
enjoying flowers:

*How marvelous the flowers are! But why don't they
resemble each other? The rose is the most beautiful,
and gives off a fragrant scent; the others are not as
lovely, and yet they all grow in the same earth.* [29]

Her father explained that the rose was the image of all that was brilliant
on earth. She was proud; the queen of flowers. But, her reign was
short. The slightest wind caused her to fade; she lasted but a day.
Other flowers, less lovely, did not fade as fast. The ephemeral quality
of beauty stressed by St-Gervais was meant to discourage young girls
from spending too much time in front of the mirror.

Peigné explained that vanity frequently led to another common female
failing, tardiness. In a story called, *"Mademoiselle En Retard"* [30] the
young woman was repeatedly late because she spent too much time
primping. This in turn disrupted the schedule of others, particularly of
men who had important work to do.

In contrast, the good qualities described in several stories emphasized
the courage of boys who didn't let themselves be distracted from
their duty regardless of what they missed. Boys who learned to bear the
difficulties of life and who knew that work gets us everything we want.

"Work is a treasure." Men's work, unlike women's work, was described as important to society. Farming, building, mining and weaving were all necessary jobs which men performed for the benefit of all. Their reward:

> *And for you, brave little man,*
> *For you, the right to be happy....* [31]

Since women's work was not viewed as difficult, but rather as natural, they shouldn't expect such rewards. The spheres outlined for the girls were not only separate, but clearly unequal. The adult roles which were being inculcated were not realistic. Many mothers had to work to help feed their families and hence couldn't be home to devote themselves day and night to their children. But the girls were learning that this was the appropriate behavior for a mother, this was the role they should aspire to. This ideal family image was reinforced by the poem: "Those I Love."

> *I love Mama, who promises and gives*
> *So many kisses to her child.*
> *And who so quickly forgives him*
> *Whenever he is naughty!*
>
> *I love Papa, who all week along*
> *Goes to work to bring me food,*
> *And who seems not to have any more worries*
> *When I bring him a good report card.* [32]

If a young working class girl wanted to learn how to achieve this ideal family life she only had to read the story of *"Cécile et Julie."* [33] Cécile and Julie, fourteen-years-old, were cousins just apprenticed to a seamstress in Paris.

Julie was the daughter of a coal seller. Her parents were courageous; though they earned little, they economized and were always solvent. Julie was brought up with religious principles and good conduct. Cécile, on the other hand, learned only dance. Her father was a musician in a cabaret where her mother also worked. Their plan for Cécile to have a glorious career in the opera was thwarted when both parents died in a brawl. Cécile went to live with Julie.

Julie proved to be a very hard working apprentice, and quickly became a skillful seamstress. Cécile was very inattentive and often was the cause of delay for her mistress. On Sundays, Cécile dressed up coquettishly. She always wanted to look better than her cousin. Cécile particularly admired jewelry and loved to stop and stare at the fancy shops.

One Sunday, in front of a jewelry store, a young man asked the girls if they would accept a gift. Julie was embarrased at the suggestion and said no. Cécile turned on her cousin:

> *Bah! you are too straight-laced; if he is rich and generous, why not accept his gift? Maybe he'll want to marry one of us. We are at the age which pleases; I have read that love at first sight lasts a lifetime.* 34

July replied that she didn't read novels and didn't expect anything but work and prudent conduct for her future.

But Cécile had been poorly educated. She had read that a poor girl need only be young and pretty to captivate hearts; thus she believed, like many others, that she could win her fortune by not neglecting her looks. Cécile had the wrong idea not only from bad novels, but also from the theatre which she had gone to with her mother. There she saw poor girls find rich men who fell in love and married. She also saw actresses from humble origins covered with furs and jewels. She got used to the practice of women accepting gifts from men. Cécile arranged a secret meeting with the young man and disappeared.

Julie replied that she didn't read novels and didn't expect anything but few years she gave her parents great joy by bringing home her weekly pay. After her parents died, Julie helped an old, sick neighbor until he died. Meanwhile, Jacques Duval, a good-hearted, young man of thirty, took over the coal shop and after a few months, Julie and Jacques married and started a family. The coal shop prospered due to the order in their private lives.

After several years passed, Julie received a letter from Cécile who lay dying in a hospital. Cécile wrote:

> *My bad conduct brought me to this deplorable situa-*
> *tion.... I will die with less bitterness if I can have your*
> *forgiveness....* '' 35

Julie and Jacques brought home the repentant sinner. In their home she learned that there was no greater happiness than living with a unified family with virtue the only rule of conduct. Cécile married Philippe, one of Jacques' good workers and the four of them lived happily.

Following this story the author underlined the moral by reminding the young readers that bad conduct resulted in sickness and death while hard work (within appropriate spheres) led to happiness and good fortune. This was the lesson which the teachers hoped to impress on the minds of their pupils. Girls shouldn't dream of instant fortune, but should remember Julie's patience, hard work, caring for parents, her neighbor, and later her own husband and children.

The above stories provide additional evidence of the attempt to impose modern consciousness on the women workers of Lyon and their daughters. In advice columns from reformers, in church and at school the segregation of work from family life was constantly reinforced. It is significant that this modern view which gradually came to dominate all institutions was bourgeois in origin and was not accepted without a struggle.

Robert Colls, in a study of the schools created for English coal miners' children, pointed out that the educational process was really a "massive exercise in trying to shift the nascent loyalties of children away from the community which would nurture them and the men and women who had borne them." 36 Likewise, the schools in Lyon were one aspect of an ongoing struggle for cultural hegemony waged between artisans and workers on one hand and merchants and manufacturers on the other. Some women workers set up schools to rival those run by the religious orders. Housing no more than 10 to 20 pupils, scores of these schools were denounced by inspectors as mere baby-sitting operations. 37 It is quite likely that these schools were criticized because they were part of the workers' community. These schools which evolved out of the needs of working women, rather than the needs of bourgeois employers, did not try to impose new standards.

Mme. Stumpf's class of 65 indigent pupils who met in her home was one of those schools merely tolerated by the Croix-Rousse municipal authorities. [38] When she urged the mayor to subsidize her school so that she could provide a good education for her girls, she was told instead to reduce the number of pupils she accepted. Mme. Stumpf also held free classes at night for adults. Unlike the religious orders, her efforts went unfunded.

Despite the appeal of the dames' school traditional approach, the overwhelming superiority of classroom, equipment, books, and prizes, made the religious schools far more attractive. Even parents who wished to preserve artisanal culture were assaulted by the rising affluence of the bourgeoisie, and lured by the constant refrain of "get rich" (*"enrichissez-vous"*). These parents increasingly sent their daughters to schools run by holy orders.

Chapter VI

MOTHERS AND DAUGHTERS: GENERATION GAP IN THE ATELIER

The gradual demise of the family workshop as an economic institution was accompanied by the emergence of a new type of family which developed sex-specific roles still prevalent in the twentieth century. The triumph of large capitalist workshops described above forced the children of artisan households to leave their atelier in search of work for wages. Simultaneously the bourgeois ideas of individualism, progress, work, thrift, order, social mobility, and a narrowly-defined sphere for women replaced an older mentality which was less and less useful in a world changed by the capitalist organization of labor.

Children who grew up in the family workshops of the July Monarchy learned from their parents an artisanal set of values and skills but also came into contact with new work places, and new ideas imposed by the bourgeois-dominated school and church. They brought the new mentality home to parents whose views had been formulated during the more prosperous years of the Restoration. The artisanal values of the pre-industrial era were often neither conscious nor expressed. To get a glimpse at them we must look closely at the evidence which remains of life in the atelier.

Most artisans during the Old Regime set up their workshops in St. Georges, on the right bank of the Saône. The artisan population shifted during the July Monarchy to the Croix-Rousse hilltops which accommodated a burgeoning population. After 1850 the greatest growth was on the left bank of the Rhône where the proletariat of Lyon concentrated.[1]

A close look at the St. Georges quarter revealed dwellings with low ceilings connected by subterranean passages and extremely narrow streets paved with little stones which were perpetually muddy and garbage-strewn. Villermé described these homes as amongst the most overcrowded and unsanitary in Europe. [2] From 1820, those *canuts* who could afford 350 francs per year left the city for the new buildings constructed on the Croix-Rousse hillside. [3] There they found homes with ceilings tall enough (nine and a half to eleven feet), [4] to accommodate the new Jacquard silk looms; there they were also able to escape from the high duty (the *octroi*) on meat and wine imposed on residents of the city but not on those who lived in the Croix-Rousse which remained a suburb of Lyon until it was annexed in 1851; [5] and finally, living on the Croix-Rousse brought them closer to the open fields where children could play and families could picnic on Sunday afternoons.

From the size and lay-out of the flats on the Croix-Rousse we can learn something about the traditional family workshops of the early nineteenth century and the people who lived and worked within. Most buildings were six or seven stories high with no interior courtyard. Each story had several flats of two rooms which were often inhabited by seven people--the master craftsman (*chef d'atelier*), his wife, three children, a journeyman and an apprentice. [6]

Typically, the larger room was approximately 23' x 10'; and had three functions. Principally it was a workshop, housing four looms which were anchored to a specially reinforced floor. For about twelve hours each day these looms were operated by the master craftsman, a journeyman, an apprentice, and the master's wife. The children were often employed in running errands for the weavers and in aiding them at the loom. The air was permeated with silk dust which settled everywhere. The room generally had a window but it was often kept closed to protect the delicate silk fiber from the elements. [7]

In addition to the looms there was usually a table in this room on which the members of the household would take their meals. The benches from the looms were moved over to the table at mealtime. A stove and a small chest of dishes and utensils were often placed in a small alcove off to the side of this large room. The stove was used for cooking and also for heating the flat. Most of the dishes were rough earthenware, but many weavers had linen cloths to cover their tables, at least on Sunday.[8] At night, trundle beds stored under the table and looms were moved out to convert the room to its use as a dormitory for the children and the journeyman and apprentice. Or the group might sleep on a platform built over the table. In any case, little privacy was provided in this setting. Often small, narrow beds and blankets were shared.[9]

The second, smaller room was used by the master and his wife as a bedroom. This room generally contained a better bed and linens. A chest to contain the linens and the clothing of the family was also kept in this room. In many homes on the Croix-Rousse books were found on top of the chest and in some instances busts or pictures of Saint-Simonian leaders.[10]

The quality of life in these flats is not easy to visualize. We know that husbands and wives had to cooperate in order to start their workshop and to continue working together to make it grow. While Villermé may have exaggerated when he reported that most weavers married in order to start a workshop,[11] the converse was true: without a wife a young master would not be able to get a loan from a silk merchant to buy his first loom, nor would he be able to afford to pay a reeler to prepare the thread for the loom, a job assumed by most young wives.[12] As time went on the married weaver would teach his wife how to weave and then buy a second loom. With both of them weaving they would be able to pay someone to do the preparatory work on the silk thread. Later they would add more looms to the shop, hiring journeymen to work them. Then the wife would assume the important responsibility of feeding all the members of the household as well as working in the family enterprise.[13]

The master craftsman and his wife had to cooperate in another area as well--limiting the number of their children was important to the silk workers of the Croix-Rousse. Since a weaver's child could not earn enough money by reeling and spinning to be self-sufficient until the age of 16, many small children could ruin a weaver's family. The average number of children living in flats in the Croix-Rousse for the period 1801-1834 was 3.23. Since the *canuts* usually married between the ages of 24 and 27, and the *canutes* were 20 to 23, we must assume that they were doing something to prevent having more than three or four children. Villermé praised them for their abstinence.[14] We have no proof of this or any other method, but there are indications. We know that coitus interruptus was used increasingly in eighteenth-century France as a means of limiting the number of children in the family.[15] We must also consider the possibility that the *canutes* were conceiving but aborting, or conceiving, delivering and allowing their young to die by shipping them out to wet-nurses who were notorious for ill-care of their charges.[16] Regardless of the method, some form of cooperation between husbands and wives was necessary to achieve the desired result.[17]

Thus, despite the master craftsman's position as head of the workshop, his wife was not a mere domestic to help him with the tasks, she was rather a partner who had shared years of cooperation with her husband. In their atelier work and play, production and all the other aspects of family life went on in the same space. There was no differentiated area for "women's work." Most often, food preparation and other household chores were the responsibility of apprentices, while the wife of the master craftsman was engaged in weaving.

We have noted that the homes in the Croix-Rousse were an improvement over those in the St. Georges area and probably better than most peasant dwellings. Barring crises--prolonged illness or lack of work-- the food eaten by silk workers, the clothing they wore and the education they provided their children were all improving, though not steadily. In good times, the master and his family ate white bread and cheese for breakfast while the journeyman ate plain bread. The master sometimes added coffee and milk to his breakfast. For dinner they had soup, sometimes thick with vegetables, sometimes clear broth, followed by meat and vegetables and potatoes or salad. The master and his family enjoyed a bottle of wine (half to one liter per day) with their dinner. For supper, leftovers from dinner and a little extra salad. In 1836, Villermé was impressed by the fact that the silk workers ate much better than the majority of French workers.[18]

With regard to clothing, the silk workers were much better off than the peasantry. They had colored cottons for summer and broadcloth for winter. They wore shoes all year round. They had special dress for work and for holidays. Many observers felt that it was difficult to tell them apart from the bourgeoisie when they were gathered for parties.[19]

The cohesive and prosperous family workshop of the Restoration was not immune to the technological and economic developments of the industrial revolution. First, there was the massive change to hiring rural weavers for simple silks which began as a response to the uprisings of 1831 and 1834 and continued through mid-century.[20] As we have described, silk merchants also began buying expensive machinery, well beyond the reach of the artisan weavers, which they installed in workshops of 40-50 weaver employees.[21] Instead of investing money in new factory buildings, many of these businessmen financed workshops within the numerous convents surrounding Lyon. Gradually more and more weaving was done in large shops owned by the merchants on looms owned by merchants, at times dictated by merchants, and for wages determined by merchants.[22] The artisan and his workshop experienced these changes with bewilderment and a desire to restore conditions, to return to the "good old days."

> *We have not always been so miserable; it isn't our fault; in the days when good workers could earn enough by working we had blouses and linens, now we have pawned them to pay the rent.*[23]

They were distressed by the uncertainty of the future and the inability to plan for their children's security.

In 1844 Flora Tristan visited one old weaver who had raised a large family during the 1820's when his work had been well paid. He had taught all of his children to weave and now they were all in miserable conditions.[24]

The worsening economic conditions of the artisan silk weavers made them resort to demands for minimum prices for their work. They urged an end to the increasing use of convent workers and unskilled countryside weavers. They were particularly opposed to their wives being employed in factories where artisans were not opposed to their wives working, but they wanted them to continue to work at home in the atelier.

The social order which the master weavers tried to protect was waning due to capitalist industrialization. In many cases artisan husbands and wives and children were no longer working at home, they were

86

employees, hired by capitalists. Their social roles had changed despite the fact that they had not yet accepted the change in their system of beliefs. Some of the family workshops founded in the 1820's and the 1830's continued to eke out a marginal existence. When a crisis occurred and a master could no longer afford to hire a journeyman or apprentice (because the cost of feeding them was greater than the money they brought in) he let them go and his wife and children took up the slack. When hard times grew worse, they pawned the family's possessions and cut back on food.

Tristan interviewed another *canut* family, a mother, father, and three children, in the Croix-Rousse. They had a one-room flat which served as kitchen, bedroom and workshop for two looms. The husband wove at one loom and his wife at the other. Working an 18-hour day the husband earned 28-30 sous and the wife 18-20 per day. The three children did the reeling and other small tasks to help their parents. With their combined income they complained that they were unable to afford to eat anything but bread. They could not pay to have their clothing washed. The family and everything in the flat was covered with dust from the silk. The husband was tired and sickly from overwork. The wife, who had given birth to eight children, five of whom had already died of misery and overwork, expressed the wish that death would come to relieve her soon. [25] Having been taught that they had freedom to manage their own lives, many workers undoubtedly saw their failure as personal.

Others did not. In a neighboring flat, a single room served as bedroom, kitchen, and workshop. One window provided light and ventilation. The husband sat at one loom and the wife at the second. The husband was almost naked because his only shirt was hung on the window to dry from perspiration. The wife clutched 20-30 yellow sheets, pawn tickets from the Mont de Piété. This couple had pawned their blouses and linens to pay for rent, heat and light. They worked side by side, 18 hours per day, in a state of perpetual exhaustion and were not even able to buy anything to eat besides bread. [26] The husband and wife were driven desperate by their conditions. They had reached the point where they preferred to die fighting, rather than die of hunger. The weakened husband repeated, pathetically, several times, "I am prepared to descend to the public square and to fight." [27]

Other masters looked to different solutions. Many must have reluctantly followed the route taken by M. Verne who broke from the traditional workshop, left his loom to his wife and took a job as a day laborer at which he could earn more money.[28] Others who reached the point of utter desperation saw suicide as the only way out. The *Echo de la Fabrique* carried this news story on June 15, 1844:

LACK OF WORK, MISERY, SUICIDE

M. Brosse, a master craftsman, who has been profoundly depressed for a long time because of the lack of work, and because his wife has been ill for a long time, has just committed suicide. ... He jumped into the Saône. This unhappy man left two young children. [29]

The event was reported in all the Lyonese newspapers, but seventeen days after the suicide, no help had come to the ailing widow or the small children.

Children whose artisan traditions were broken early were more easily socialized as proletarians. M. Brosse's children were unlikely to grow up in an artisan family workshop. Sickly widows with no economic assets could hardly expect to remarry. In 1843, for example, while 175 widowers married single women, only 103 single men married widows in the Croix-Rousse.[30] Widows frequently had no secure residence; many experienced downward social mobility.

The story of the widow Pila was a case in point. Mme. Pila appeared before the Chamber of Appeals of the Correctional Police of Lyon and told the judge that she could not take custody of her son, who had been brought in on a minor charge.[31] She explained that she had no permanent home, no food and no means of existence. She could not reclaim her son, because she had no job. She repeated several times that it was a great humiliation for her to admit these facts and that she wished to arrange to come for her son as soon as possible.

Touched by the scene of a mother unable to take care of her son, someone in the room agreed to take care of the boy temporarily and the Court agreed to postpone its ruling. Some men in the courtroom took up a collection to aid Pila out of her immediate misery. But, no commitments were made, no jobs offered, no long-range plans volunteered.

In another case a widow was the victim of the legal system. Mme. Ch's husband died in the hospital, a disgusting place which contained 1500 sick people crammed into filthy wards. [32] After his death on September 10, 1845, his widow claimed his belongings which had a possible value of 20-25 francs. The hospital administration refused to give them to her on the grounds that she had no official proof that she was his heir. In order to prove her rights she would have to spend 12-15 francs--a sum which she did not have--on a judicial proceeding. Despite repeated efforts, two months later the hospital was still holding on to the belongings. [33]

The children of these widows whose families were disrupted by death and dislocation were apt to join the workers who saw their position as a personal failing, who were not determined to fight for higher salaries. These workers asked for reductions in the price of bread arguing, "We are nothing but workers." [34]

Despite the economic uncertainties, boys and girls growing up in artisan workshops tried to create their own family shop when they married. A study of the first fifty marriages recorded in the Croix-Rousse in 1834, 1844, and 1854 [35] produced compelling evidence that despite the sharp competition from rural weavers and merchant-manufacturers, men and women continued to marry and set up family workshops through mid-century. The Croix-Roussians who married in these years fell into three categories: those who had grown up in work-shops, those who had grown up on farms and those for whom we have no information.

Children who had been socialized in a family workshop would have had a difficult time envisioning a family that was not based in their own atelier. For them family meant working together--husband and wife and in time children and apprentices--in their own flat with their own tools. In other words, family was synonymous with family workshop. In striking contrast, the silk workers whom they saw employed by a master or by an entrepreneur were almost exclusively single. The journeyman's Ferrandinier union even specified that membership was limited to single men. [36] Being single and being employed by somebody else in their shop thus seemed to go together, while marriage implied the stability of a family workshop.

Similarly for the rural raised young men and women family was tied up with the notion of working together for a common goal to eke out a living on a small plot. Often single men and women were sent out of their families to work for someone else to help the family economy. But marriage entailed setting up a home and work unit. For the farmer's children, like the artisan's, the family was primarily an economic unit. When they moved to the city the transition from family farm to family workshop seemed natural.

The marriage records tell us quite a bit about these "inarticulate" people. Since physical needs and economic preparedness did not always coincide, it was not surprising to learn from the 1844 marriage records that twenty percent of the couples studied were already living together at the time of their marriage, and that eight percent were legitimizing children who had been born earlier (in most cases two- to four-year-old children, but one case of a fifteen-year-old girl was also mentioned). Thus it was clear that sexual union and even having children were not sufficient reasons for marriage in the artisan culture. Couples often lived together to satisfy physical and emotional needs but in most cases did not marry until they could set up their own shop.

Further evidence of this sytem were the abortions practiced by women silk workers, the large numbers of abandoned children, and even infanticides. [37] Couples who had lived together with the intention of marrying when they had saved sufficient money often changed their plans when protracted unemployment wiped out their savings. In this instance a child often became an unbearable liability for the single woman who was left alone to fend for herself and her baby. [38]

Since silk workers had to wait until they had sufficient capital to marry-- to rent their workshop and looms--it is not surprising to learn that the median age at marriage went up to 27 for men and 26 for women in 1834 and stayed the same in 1844. By 1854, the age for men went up to 29 and remained the same for women. Even more significant is the very wide range of ages at which couples married for the first time; from the late teens to the sixties, suggesting that economic rather than emotional or physical needs often determined marital age. Finally 24% of the marriages in 1834, 26% in 1844, and 20% in 1854 were between younger men and older women, suggesting that brides were often highly valued for the amount of money that they could bring to the marriage.

A glance at one of the silk worker couples marrying in 1844 illustrates some of the reasons behind these marriages. Philibert Bejuge, twenty-four-years-old, and Jeanne Morel, twenty-six-years-old, married on January 27. Neither had inherited a family workshop. The fathers of both bride and groom had died when their children were very young (nine and ten respectively). Since their mothers were listed as day workers, it is fair to assume that Philibert and Jeanne had to amass their skills and capital on their own. The record reveals that the couple were already living at the same address: rue de Chapeaux Rouge 19, and already had a son, Hughes, who was almost two years old. Though the couple had been living together for at least two and one-half years they remained unmarried until they could afford to set up their own family workshop.[39]

The extensive testimony of Norbert Truquin about his marriage and the difficulties of setting up a family workshop in the late fifties are illustrative of the problems faced by artisans who did not want to give up their way of life.[40] At the time of his marriage, Truquin had a small apartment, big enough for his two looms, and fifty francs saved. His wife came to the marriage with 200 francs she had saved while working for another master craftsman as a weaver. Truquin purchased the utensils he needed for setting up his two looms for 600 francs, putting down 200 francs, and agreeing to pay the remainder in four installments at three-month intervals. But two months after the marriage work ceased completely and the couple remained without any work for the next six months. As a result Truquin had to ask for extensions on his loans and he and his wife were forced to beg for bread and credit from the baker and grocer respectively. He and his wife lived on potatoes and bread for six months.

Truquin recorded in his diary that he had married in order to raise a family. And that he began to do almost immediately. Within the first year of marriage his wife gave birth, but this was not the happy occasion they had hoped for since it took place at the same time that Truquin and his wife were evicted from their apartment for failing to pay the rent. His wife was forced, much to her chagrin, to give birth in a hospital.[41]

Despite these obstacles, in a short time Truquin and his wife were able to set up a new family workshop in different quarters in the

Croix-Rousse. In these new surroundings Truquin and his wife and children and their artisan neighbors perpetuated the system which emphasized the association between family and family workshop.

In addition to the artisan families described above, there were also many marriages where no workshop was set up, where husbands and wives continued to be employed outside of their home; these latter are the first proletarian families. In 1834, 24 out of the 50 marriages studied could be categorized as proletarian; ten years later, 19 out of the 50 and in 1854, 14 out of 50 (see chart below). [42]

	Artisan Families	Proletarian Families	No Information
1834	26	24	0
1844	28	19	3
1854	31	14	5

In most cases, the proletarian marriage partners are themselves the products of proletarian families; that is, the son or daughter of an unskilled worker is likely to register as a day laborer or domestic. Or they might be the sons or daughters of farmers who have put geographic distance and probably several years between themselves and their families and have been able to change their traditional concept of family life. Out of the 150 marriages studied over a thirty-year period, there were only three cases of children who grew up in a family workshop in Lyon who did not marry with the intent to set one up themselves. [43] It is likely that the progeny of the artisans who were unsuccessful in accumulating the required sums to set up an atelier remained single or emigrated from Lyon and married elsewhere.

It is important to note that all of the masters did not experience downward social mobility. The following account of the Bellin family was illustrative of the upward social mobility experienced by some and hoped for by most weaving families. [44] On February 20, 1834, Louis Dominique Bellin, a thirty-eight-year-old weaver from rural Cusset, married Benoite Montely, a twenty-eight-year-old weaver born in Lyon. The marriage was registered in the Croix-Rousse where they were already living together with their seven-year-old daughter, Adèle. How and where Louis and Benoite met remained obscure. But their long cohabitation, fortunately for the historian, was pretty clear. On March 14, 1827 (when Benoite was twenty-one and Louis thirty-one) a daughter Adèle had been born and registered in La Guillotière, a rural suburb of Lyon.

It was not unusual for weavers to have illegitimate children and to legitimize them several years later. (In 1844, four of the first fifty marriages registered in the Croix-Rousse legitimized children.) The Bellins were probably unable to afford to set up a workshop until 1834 and, therefore, postponed marriage for several years. When they married, their first workshop was on the third floor of 26 Rue des Fosses, it had two rooms and they paid 180 frs rent per year. They had two fancy looms in it and one female apprentice lived with them. One year later the Bellin family fortune declined. They moved to a one-room flat where they paid only 80 frs. rent per year. The female apprentice was still with them but they no longer had the looms. Instead they had one reeling machine.

In 1837 the family fortune improved dramatically. They moved to a two-room flat and had six looms--three for simple silk, three for fancy. The apprentice was replaced by two workers. Their daughter Adèle registered at a Sisters of St. Charles school for artisans' daughters.

During the next six years the Bellin family specialized in fancy weaving only; they sold three simple looms and acquired a fourth fancy loom. The decision was apparently fortunate since the census taken in 1843 noted the family condition as comfortable (aisé). By 1845 the Bellins paid 250 frs rent and hired two women workers and two apprentices. The same year their daughter married Joseph Joubert, a twenty-five-year-old weaver who lived in Lyon.

Adèle Bellin differed in three significant ways from her mother Benoite Montely: she had no child to legitimize at her marriage, she was only eighteen-years-old compared to her mother who had been twenty-eight; she signed her name while her mother did not; she recorded "no profession" (which was a category reserved for young women of bourgeois standing) while her mother was a weaver. Further indication of the upward social mobility of the Bellin family was the use of the prefixes "Sieur" and "Dame" when referring to Adèle's parents in the marriage record.

For the Bellin family and others who were able to improve their status it was easy to believe that their achievements were due to individual initiative, hard work, and good living. They agreed with the editors of *Nouvel Echo de la Fabrique* that the emancipation of the working class depends on two points: physical improvement and moral improvement. Language, manners, habits all should be "comme il faut."[45] The lessons of Adèle's teachers fell on receptive ears at the Bellin household.

This family did not look back nostalgically to the good old days. They probably would have approved of the arrest in 1847 of five women who were caught singing this song:

> *Marry your daughters at fifteen,*
> *The white flag will return.*
> *The white flag, the fleur de lys,*
> *We will see it again soon.* [46]

Benoite Montely encouraged her daughter to look to the future not to the past.

Thus, the traditions of the artisan family of Lyon emblazoned on their banners in 1831 and 1834--*"Vivre en travaillant or mourir en combattant"*--passed slowly from the scene. The right to continue living and working in the family workshop was lost in the battle with industrialization. Those families who were successful in adapting their skills to the changing technology and growing financial power of Lyon succumbed to *embourgeoisement,* and the others to proletarianization. In both groups the home was no longer the center of production, but rather the refuge from production and the marketplace. The family as Christopher Lasch pointed out, became a center of a new kind of emotional life, a new intimacy and inwardness [47] which were to be the boundaries of woman's activities.

In 1843, Louis Vasbenter, a Lyonese artisan, expressed it this way:

> *Woman's life is the life of the home, of the domestic,*
> *the interior life. Not that I pretend she must serve as a*

slave her master, not that she be entirely submissive to the wants of men.... By her new education, by greater instruction that will make her the equal of man, she will exercise on him a legitimate and salutary influence; and her ideas will hardly ever differ from her tutor; it will not be subjegating her if man represents her to the outside world. [48]

Workers accepted this limited sphere for women and the other bourgeois values because they appeared to be effective; hard work seemed to bring rewards to a minority and those who failed increasingly blamed themselves. When Karl Marx urged workers to unite--"you have nothing to lose but your chains"--he looked beyond their hopes for individual social mobility within the bourgeois order, hopes which were central to their lives.

These hopes were fostered by the family; nurtured by mothers and fathers for their children. Nineteenth century craftsmen who no longer trained their children to follow in their footsteps because there was no longer any family craft to pass on, encouraged their children to practice the new "virtues," motivating them to go to school, to be neat and clean, to be punctual. Mothers hoped their daughters would be able to report on their marriage act "sans profession."

Chapter VII

UNITY AND EQUALITY FOR WHOM?

The triumph of the bourgeoisie was not won easily. While not always recognizing subtle shifts in mentality engineered by priests, teachers and reformers, workers responded to the obvious changes in work and working conditions. Pamphlets protesting the new conditions began to circulate in Paris and in Lyon as early as 1833. These pamphlets reflected many of the problems which faced the emerging working class--low wages, unemployment, a rapidly expanding labor force, alienation from their work, and isolation in the cities. But, none of them dealt directly with the growing numbers of women workers who were employed away from home outside of the traditional family income.

Grignon, a tailor, argued that workers were forced to work for too many hours and for too meager a wage in *Les Réflexions d'un tailleur sur la misère des ouvriers en général.* He also discussed the deteriorating relationships between master craftsmen and their workers, and concluded that there was a need for worker associations to seek solutions to these problems. [1] But, Grignon neglected the significant controversy between tailors and seamstresses with regard to the items that each were restricted to sew.

A type-setter, Jules Leroux, was convinced that the main problem confronting workers was not wages or hours, but the lack of relationships between fellow workers. In *Aux Ouvriers Typographes* he reasoned that this isolation was a result of the French Revolution which theoretically guaranteed freedom for the workers, but this only meant freedom from each other. [2] As a result, when a worker was in a bad position, no one felt obliged to come to his aid. The same was true for master craftsmen. If one of them needed a little help to prevent bankruptcy, his fellows ignored him. He was forced to sell at the lowest possible prices, losing his shop and his tools, firing his journeymen, and joining the swelling ranks of workers himself. [3]

Leroux concluded that the working class did not exist; there were only individual workers. Each one entered his shop alone, without inquiring from whence came his shop-mates. They all had unequal talents, but did not try to learn from each other. They knew that once past the shop door they all were equally insignificant in the eyes of the employer and that the one most clever at intrigue, not the best worker, would succeed in bettering himself. Thus, skills became unimportant, and holding on to the job was the only goal. A worker who dared to question the poor craftsmanship of a fellow was challenged: "Will you feed me and my family?" [4]

This feeling of isolation from one's fellows and lack of pride in one's work was aggravated by a swelling work force. Steadily decreasing wages encouraged fathers to teach their children their trades at an earlier age and to dump them into the work force so as to increase the family's total income. Machines did away with the need for skills, and in some cases for workers, adding to the congestion in other jobs. [5]

French workers were left with three possible paths to follow: they could intrigue on an individual basis for the chance of individual rewards; they could remain isolated in an ever growing sea of workers; or they could unite to pursue collective ends. Leroux advocated unity. But, even though he recognized the crushing problem of isolation, he failed to include the most isolated of all the workers--the women-- in his plans for union.

A third pamphleteer, Efrahem, a shoemaker, advocated an association of male workers of all trades. In his book, *De l'Association des ouvriers de tous les corps d'état,* subtitled *Union et force,* he reasoned that a general association gathered strength from all the trades, whereas if they remained separate, they remained weak. His plan called for the members of each trade to get together and choose representatives to work out wages with the masters. Each group would correspond with the others to arrange for a central committee which would create a central bank whose funds would be used to support striking workers. [6]

Despite his energetic rhetoric, Efrahem's notion of unity--like those of his predecessors--neglected women workers. One of the main concerns expressed in his pamphlet was for male workers to earn enough money to support their wives and children at home. [7] This concern was a leitmotif for all the men's demands for higher wages. It was restated conclusively in 1842 by the workers' journal, *L'Atelier*, "We (the editors) believe that the condition of women cannot be improved until (men) workers earn enough money to support their whole family--that alone is justice." [8]

But, the fact was that working men did not earn enough to support their wives at home and increasing numbers of women--both married and single--joined the labor force. In Lyon, we noted that the *canutes* made up 70% of the silk labor force; yet, even they were not included in the many plans for union drawn up by the artisan silk weavers. [9] Union members in Lyon were a complex potpourri: old-time political radicals who adhered to Babouvist methods; Saint-Simonians whose social ideas were now tempered with Enfantin's mysticism; utopian socialists who followed Fourier, Proudhon, or Cabet; skilled craftsmen; and country lads who came to work in the silk industry, derisively known as *carmagnoles*.

Despite the obvious differences in education and skills, these men began to realize that they had much in common. Living in close proximity to each other they saw that they all shared cold, hunger, exhaustion, chronic ill-health. Drinking together in the same taverns, they were aware that they shared the fears of unemployment, of insecurity in the face of old age, and the terrors of isolation in a city bustling with people. Gradually they began to feel an identity of interests amongst themselves and against their enemy the bourgeoisie, more specifically their capitalist employers. But this feeling did not encompass their wives and mothers and daughters, though they clearly shared the same falling standard of living and the same insecurity about their jobs. Thus, when artisans and *carmagnoles*, radicals and utopians, began to articulate their identity of interests by calling themselves the working class in Lyon in the 1830's and '40's they really meant the male working class.

Similarly, it is very important not to misunderstand the rhetoric of "unity and equality" omnipresent in the worker press of this period. Unity and equality was to be limited only to male workers. In 1844, for example, Devaux, a silk weaver from the Croix-Rousse, wrote a song in which he called on workers--"proletaires"[10] --to unite against the common enemy. But it was clear from the verse that follows that he was referring to men workers only:

> *Alert! Proletariat,*
> *We will vanquish our enemies,*
> *If like good brothers*
> *We know how to unite.*

What about the good "sisters" who were also being exploited? Here again women workers were not accounted for. The song continued with the assurance that "when equality would be reborn, the reign of iniquity would disappear."[11] But, Devaux clearly did not refer to equality in terms of wages for men and women workers doing the same jobs; he still thought in abstract political terms. Since the sharp disparity between men's and women's wages was one of the most successful ways the silk businessmen had to exploit their workers, Devaux's conclusion that "our exploiters will be more conciliating" was a mere pipe dream.

Throughout our period, the *canuts* continued to oppose the principle of paying women the same wages as men for doing the same job. They continued to cling to the idea that women were basically inferior to men and therefore could not do men's work. They ignored the fact that much of their work was simplified because of the introduction of new machines and that lengthy apprenticeships to highly skilled professions were not required for producing mixed fabrics. the *canuts* also believed that women had fewer needs than men and therefore should be paid less. [12]

Thus, the persistence of traditional ideas about the inferiority of women effectively divided the Lyonese labor force into two groups--the *canuts* who demanded higher wages and the *canutes* who accepted a woman's wage. The fact that the men failed to recognize the women as equally capable and therefore deserving of equal pay acted as a barrier to working class solidarity, and ironically this thwarted their own ability to obtain higher wages from their employers. The consciousness of the working class was not limited to the observation that they were being exploited. They understood the mechanism used by their employers to exploit them--i.e., employing their wives and daughters at half-wages. But they refused to accept women workers as equals and persisted in trying to remove them from the labor force.

This was partly due to the heritage of the traditional relationship between men and women which stemmed from a peasant society based on the patriarchal family. In peasant families, women were sub-ordinated to their husbands, who were respected for performing the heavy physical work which women could not do. Because the husband was the main provider, he had certain rights. For example, he always ate first while his wife stood nearby to serve him. When he finished, the wife served whatever hired help he had, and finally, ate the leftovers when all the men had finished. [13]

As we have seen, this unequal relationship was buttressed by the influence of priests, teachers, and reformers who sought to restrict women's sphere to the home. In the city the wife of a master craftsman often ate the lesser share--quality and quantity, and wore the poorer clothes, the finer being reserved for their artisan husbands. Likewise it was the husbands who spent money in the local taverns while their wives remained at home. [14] Men workers, whether they were of recent peasant origin or fifth generation craftsmen, shared the idea that men should rule their own roost, that they should be the major breadwinner, and that their wives must be subservient to them. Although more and more women were being employed outside of their homes, and paid a direct wage by their employers, their time-honored role of subserv-ience, modified by the bourgeois idea of domesticity, remained dominant especially in the minds of the husbands.

But some women argued that men could no longer support them because there were not enough men in the city to marry all of them. If they were forced to remain single, they would have to support them-selves. Further, the *canutes* who married complained that many of their husbands were unemployed and that they were forced to support their whole families on their woman's wage. Women with sick husbands and widows also complained that as sole breadwinners for their families they should receive higher wages.[15] Essentially these women argued that new conditions had forced them to become an important, or the sole, breadwinner for themselves and their families. Therefore, they demanded to be paid a living wage and the right to join worker clubs which provided sick pay and pensions.

But men workers were convinced that women suffered from illness more often than men and would therefore be a drain on their union's budgets. Further, they questioned how women could pay the same dues and acquire the same benefits as men when they earned half the wages. The *canuts* also feared that the labor force was expanding too rapidly and that growing numbers of *canutes* would bring down the price of labor. As a result, they denied women membership in all their societies and clubs, and demanded that their members actively exclude women from their trade.[16]

The right of workers to limit the number of people practicing their profession was a tradition dating back to the corporations of the Old Regime. The corporations were semi-autonomous bodies which could prevent non-members from practicing their craft primarily by refusing to train them and license them.[17] In order to become a member of the corporation one had to serve three to four years of apprenticeship, and to pay an entrance fee which varied from 20 to 30 livres. The position of master (or mistress in the few exclusively female corporations) was generally reserved for the son of the master who had to pay large sums to buy the post.[18]

But, the *canuts* of the 1840's were not working under the same conditions as the artisans of the Old Regime. They were faced with growing numbers of *canutes* who were already trained (by their husbands to work at home) and could be employed without any special license. By excluding the *canutes* from their clubs they did not exclude them from the work force, they merely left them to contend with the job market without any clubs or unions to act as buffer. This was especially ironic when one considers the high value--at least in the rhetoric of the period--placed on union.

Excluded from the mutual-aid societies, women had to choose between remaining isolated individuals in a hostile world of insecurity and daily misery or to try to form their own societies. Women workers, traditionally subservient, uneducated, and inarticulate, were uniquely disadvantaged in organizational abilities. Their wages were so low that it was virtually impossible for them to pay dues into a common fund which would provide compensation in times of unemployment or illness. It is thus not surprising that there are no records of female mutual-aid societies in Lyon before 1848; and no women's strikes, unions or cooperatives from 1851-1869. [19]

The best organized of the worker groups of the 1830's and 1840's were not the mutual-aid societies which were geared primarily toward immediate problems, but rather the ancient *compagnonnage* system, which was an outgrowth of the various brotherhoods of builders: stone-cutters, carpenters, joiners, and locksmiths. [20] During its evolution, in the fifteenth century it took on a corporative character and it became a cohesive, self-defense group of workers in the building trades. Gradually, many other crafts joined the *compannonage*. In 1834, weavers who used Jacquard looms in Lyon formed the Ferrandinier branch, by 1841 their membership reached 3,000. [21] The elitist artisan tradition of this society and, specifically, its total exclusion of women from regular membership, were very influential factors in the development of the working class in Lyon and in all of France.

During the early 1840's there were several attempts to reform the *compagnonnage* system by its members. Adolphe Boyer, a type-setter, argued that the organization of work was necessary to the future of society and could be put into practice immediately. [22] He called for an end to the fighting among workers, and cooperation between the *compagnonnage* and the Conseil des Prud'hommes in order to organize work, but he never mentioned women workers. Unable to bear the failure of his reform efforts, Boyer committed suicide in 1843. [23]

Agricol Perdiguier, a carpenter by trade, called Arignonnais-la-Vertu [24] by his fellow *compagnons*, wrote *Le Livre du Compagnonnage*, in which he recorded all the old myths and rituals of *compagnons*, which he was eager to preserve. He was, however, anxious to put and end to the bickering among rival trades and wanted all *compagnons* to have access to culture. He envisaged a building containing a school of

102

design, a museum of famous men, and a library, in each city. [25] This grandoise project likewise failed to address the role of women workers in the new evolving industrial system.

In 1842, a blacksmith, Gosset, published, *Projet tendant a régénérer le compagnonnage sur le tour de France* in which he revealed that most of the *compagnons'* meetings resulted in drunken brawls, because of the system of fines which forced any member who disturbed a meeting to pay a fine of a bottle of wine. [26] Each time a member left a city to continue his education was another excuse to empty the treasury to buy wine for all the members. In order to ameliorate these abuses, Gosset suggested 14 rules with 107 articles, none of which considered the problem caused by employers who replaced men workers with women.

Pierre Moreau, a locksmith from Auxerre, was the only one of this group who thought the *compagnonnage* system to be too corrupted for reform to be of any use. He advocated a complete reorganization, dropping all the trade and historic divisions between groups and creating a new system which he called *L'Union.*

Moreau recognized the brotherhood of workers: "Workers, we shouldn't help each other only because we are in the same trade, but because we are all workers, all in the same social category." [27] He saw the problem caused by the elitism of the *compagnonnage* and tried to put an end to it through his Union. But on the subject of women workers, who logically were part of that same social category, he also was mute. Thus, neither the sytem of *compagnonnage,* nor any of its would be reformers, offered any solutions to the immediate problem of women workers--securing a living wage, or to the wider problem for the whole working class caused by the employment of women at half-wages.

In the mid-forties, the persistent subservient view of women also governed the male workers' response to a reform of the *livret,* an identification booklet, instituted during the Napoleonic era, which had to be held by "every individual"--excluding women--employed by another. [28] The *livret* was prepared by the commissioner of police or the mayor at no cost to the worker, and provided the following information about him: name, age, place of birth, physical description, profession, and the name and address of his employer. The worker received his first *livret* upon completing his apprenticeship or on the request of his employer.

The *livret* had several functions. First, it was an internal passport. If a worker wanted to travel, he had to cite his last dismissal on his *livret* and indicate his destination before the police commissioner. Second, the *livret* was used as a record of credit extended on the part of the employer to the worker. Whenever a worker wanted to leave a job, he was obliged to receive his employer's signature on the *livret*, attesting to the fact that the worker owed him no money. A police stamp was affixed to the signature to prevent attempts at forgery. Third, and most significant for the Lyonese workers, every job was registered on the *livret* along with the promised wage which the worker signed after he had been paid. This was often used as legal evidence in disputes over wages.[29]

In Lyon, the growing numbers of *canutes* who were involved in litigation when their bosses failed to pay them or tried to pay less than they had promised, forced the Municipal Council to reconsider its position on *livrets* for women. The debate involved the very heart of the issue discussed above--are women of the working class who are employed for wages workers in their own right? The Lyonese council was controlled by men who argued that the only women who registered with the police were prostitutes and other women should have no official papers. The same argument was used in 1847 when a national law on *livrets* was proposed. Article one of the bill stated: "Workers of both sexes who work in factories, workshops, mines ... or who work at home for one master craftsman must have a *livret*."[30] But most French men were alarmed by this notion and challenged: "The only women to register with the police were prostitutes, how can we let our wives register?"

Despite the opposition in Lyon, the Mayor of the Croix-Rousse announced a law on July 13, 1844, which obliged masters to require *livrets* for all their employees, including women and children. Failure to comply would result in being charged with a misdemeanor.[31] The workers' journal, *L'Echo de la Fabrique*, approved this law, stating that the *livret* was no longer a sign of ability or aptitude for a profession (in which case women and children would not qualify), but simply a symbol of the bearer's right to work at any available job.[32] This was an important insight considering the *canut's* previous vain attempts to limit the silk labor force by excluding women from weavers' jobs.

The journal went one step further, they regarded the institution of *livrets* for all workers as the first step towards the organization of labor. They thought that even minors who left their parents' home to work should have a *livret*. The editors of the *Echo de la Fabrique*, who were all workers themselves, reflected an awareness that the entire work force--men, women, children, shared something in common. They expressed the consciousness that men and women, while obviously different in many respects, performed the same tasks as weavers and therefore should have an identity of interests as workers. But they stopped short of agreeing to the *canutes'* demand for equal pay for equal work.

Until 1848, the *canuts* continued to oppose the principle of equal pay for equal work and refused to admit female workers into their societies. These same *canuts* recognized that the capitalist industrial revolution had taken from them the traditions of the 'just price' and that the French Revolution had removed the system of corporations leaving them only with the freedom to compete for a job on the marketplace. They responded by forming unions which demanded a minimum wage. But, they still failed to see that their women were a part of the labor force who needed the bargaining power of a strong union too. They sent their own mothers, sisters, wives, and lovers, defenseless to the marketplace and, in so doing, aided their bosses reach their objective: equal work for less pay.

In 1848, during the heady atmosphere produced by the February revolution, men and women workers met together in the great hall of the municipal library and tried to work out a solution to their economic and social problems. During the spring months the central question of the role of women workers was hotly debated. But in June conditions worsened. The dole of bread and meat organized by the city in March to feed 30,000 workers was abruptly cancelled. [33] Meanwhile the number of unemployed workers grew and swelled the ranks of the club members meeting in the library. These meetings were now frequently disturbed by short tempers and plans deteriorated from large-scale production outlines which included men and women workers to expedient short-signed goals. The central question of the role of women workers had proven insoluble to the leadership of the *canuts* and *canutes*. Before the workers could come to any final decision, the new Cavaignac regime in an attempt to restore order, issued the following decree on July 28, 1848: "Women and children cannot be members of clubs nor attend club meetings." [34] The bourgeoisie was intent on maintaining the division between men workers, and women and children workers. In Lyon, the *canuts* and *canutes,* unable to come up with any alternative during their five months of meetings, did not object to the continued division of the working class. The opportunity to work out a lasting solution to the central problem of wages for women workers thus eluded them.

Concern for the plight of women worders did not die out completely in the next few months though--in September the *Tribune Lyonnaise* reminded its readers that in times of hardship it was the women of the proletariat who suffered most. [35] But the discussion of women's role in the working class was shelved. Questions of wages, hours, and job security for *all* workers were no longer discussed at workers' meetings. The issue of the right to work for men and women was largely ignored and men workers went back to the slogan of the thirties--*"Emancipation physique and morale de la femme."* [36] Meanwhile, women scrambled to find jobs in the Lyonese market which was beginning to come back to life.

The workers' situation did not return to the status quo ante. The events of Spring 1848 had a lasting impact on some *canutes* who recognized that they were being exploited and that the *canuts* were not prepared to back them against their common employers. They became convinced that the only chance to win small improvements in their standards was to group together into producer and consumer cooperatives of *canutes.*

One such association was called *Les Fourmis Réunies.* They were a group of seamstresses who found they could survive more cheaply as a unit than as individuals. They opened a store, a workshop and a laundry at 17 Rue de la Quarantaine, on the right bank of the Saône. [37] Like scores of similar associations, Les Fourmis had no outside source of financial support and were destined to fall under any economic pressure.

There were other women's associations which were not so vulnerable to the whims of the market because they were sponsored by bourgeois women who provided the necessary capital. The sums were often used as security for manufacturers who brought the *canutes* thread to reel or weave in their workshops. [38]

One such shop, the Association of Women Workers at 31 Rue Quarantaine was established on September 17, 1848, with an initial membership of 200 women.[39] It attempted to organize its members into productive work, to pay them regularly, to provide additional instruction for all, to settle internal disputes fairly and expeditiously, and to use their profits for the benefit of all members.

Some of the members worked at home, others in workshops. Those who worked in workshops were supervised by forewomen who were elected from the ranks of the workers in the shop and maintained their position for three-month periods and could be re-elected. A maximum of 100 workers in each workshop was permitted, and the appropriate number of forewomen was decided by a directress who was also an elected official and in charge of keeping track of all the work ordered and the assignments given to different workers. [40] The administration of the workshop by women workers elected to their posts eliminated the chance of sexual exploitation by male supervisors; also, the forewomen were unlikely to overwork or cheat their workers because they wanted to be re-elected.

Wages were paid every Saturday which solved the problems of workers who had to wait a long time to receive their wages. The lowest wage was one franc per day, the forewoman received two francs, and additional prizes were offered for the best work once each month. In addition to wages, each member also received an equal share of the net profits, distributed twice each year. Medical benefits and sick pay were also provided for each woman. [41] In this system, the women workers were able to support themselves.

This exemplary association also provided instruction in reading, writing, spelling and arithmetic every day from seven to eight in the morning or from eight to nine at night. Anyone who excelled was given the opportunity to continue her education without charge. In case of arguments between women and their directress or forewomen, a jury of seven elected members of the Association who were not involved in the case met. A majority vote decided the case promptly. The Association planned to build a crèche, a day care center, a school and a training workshop adjacent to their workshops. [42] But they were defeated in this goal by the coup d'etat of Napoleon III. None of the artisan cooperatives set up from 1848-1851 survived the coup. [43]

Under the Second Empire the family workshop remained in a permanent state of crisis caused by the thousands of rural weavers employed in the factories mushrooming around Lyon. The artisan weaver was not a proletarian who had nothing to lose from social upheaval. He had a few looms, a wife, children, apprentices. Though the majority earned only 1,100 or 1,200 francs per year, which was less than the annual wage of a metallurgist, the artisans clung to their way of life. They also continued to impose their ideas about women's role in the labor force on the workers' movement up to 1869.

Master weavers opposed strikes for higher wages or shorter hours, and reminded newcomers of their earlier failures, "we know the dangers and at times the bloody results." [44] Instead they embarked once more on ambitious producer and consumer cooperatives aimed at restoring the artisanal tradition of independence. The cooperatives were by no means designed to emancipate the workers; they were an effort to maintain the elite position of artisans in the labor force. The outspoken *Progrès* criticized: "The bourgeois is a worker who has become a capitalist, large or small, and cooperatives have the precise goal of turning all workers bourgeois." [45] But the efforts at cooperation failed to improve the conditions of the majority of *canutes*.

Leading merchants, manufacturers, members of the Chamber of Commerce of Lyon, and other city leaders, officially sanctioned the membership of women in the labor force on terms which employers had persistently fostered during the July Monarchy--equal work for less pay. In the early fifties, they created the Society for Mutual-Aid and Retirement Fund of the Silk Workers of Lyon, which they funded and managed for 50 years. Unlike the previous associations founded by *canuts* for themselves, this one admitted all men and women silk workers between the ages of 18 and 35. [46]

Previous attempts at unions of *canuts* and *canutes* faltered on the problems of supporting the women's demands for equal pay and the consequences of unequal pay--i.e., unequal dues, and unequal sick pay and pensions. The Society for Mutual-Aid and Retirement Fund did not address itself to these questions. It simply accepted the status quo and by recognizing it, reinforced it. They adopted a dues-scale to partially reflect the women's lower earning power: men workers contributed two francs per month, while women paid one and a half. Consequently, sick pay amounted to two francs per day for the men and 1.50 francs for the women for the first two months; 1.50 for the men and 1.25 for the women for the next two months; and 1 franc for men and 75 centimes for women for the next 150 days. Membership in this society remained predominantly female; by 1898, 75% of its 6,227 members were *canutes*. [47]

All women workers did not accept unequal pay. In 1869 reelers and spinners who worked an average 17-hour day for 1¼ francs, and who faced frequent unemployment, asked their employers for a minimum of two francs per day and a 16-hour work day. When their demands were not met they went out on strike. They were resisted by the combined forces of law and order and the arrival of scab labor from Italy. Albert Richard, a leader of the First Internationale in Lyon, offered the striking women support, but could only give each of the 600 strikers two francs. This was the first time that striking women were aided by the Internationale in Lyon, and the first time that Internationale meetings were addressed: "Ouvriers and Ouvrières." [48]

But most women did not join the Internationale; they maintained primary allegiance to their own families rather than to the working class. After repeated failures to be accepted as equals, there is little wonder that there was such scant enthusiasm for the Internationale amongst the *canutes*. The bourgeois ethic of woman's place was easier to accept since it asked women to remain at home rather than in the labor market. It provided working women with the hope of rapid social mobility, while socialists and communists asked them to build a new society which would be a citadel of equality and justice at some time in the future.

Chapter VIII

CONCLUSION

In 1866 French delegates to the Internationale in Geneva expressed their views on family life as follows: "Without the family the human species is only a horde of creatures, lacking function, reason, law and purpose." [1] The central economic function of the family--a group who worked together to provide food and shelter for themselves--had changed. As we have seen, the separation of work from home was accompanied by the artisan's plea to keep his income high enough to support his wife and children at home, where law and purpose would be imposed on family members. This bourgeois ideology broadcast by the schools, the church, and the media, triumphed within the very heart of the socialist opposition--the Internationale. [2]

The delegates went on to explain, "Without the family, man adrift in a vast universe is an enemy to other men...." " The spirit of "free competition", as the artisans called laissez-faire capitalism, had resulted in the alienation of one *canut* from another. Their response was to look to the family as a force to counterbalance the spirit of competition in men. The family would also provide a reason for being and a shelter for women, the weaker sex. For "without the family, woman has no reason for being, for without the family, she is only an errant being, condemned by her physical constitution to premature exhaustion." This increasingly differentiated view of men and women--men as breadwinners and women as nurturers--was posed as a universal model by the bourgeoisie, accepted by artisans and finally by workers.

The new family visualized by French leaders of the Internationale was an outgrowth of the making of the working class during the four decades spanning mid-century. It was a period characterized by the gradual demise of the artisan family workshop and its cultural milieu of the just price and family wage within an hierarchical master craftsman system. The master craftsman gradually succumbed to the powerful twin forces of laissez-faire capitalism and the promise of social mobility. As Reybaud reported in 1856, the dominant characteristic of the artisan was, "he wants to improve his position."[3] Similarly, Villermé noted that it was hard to distinguish the weaver and his family from a bourgeois family on Sunday because they both wore elaborate dress.[4]

The gains made in technology and finance in the first three decades of the nineteenth century presented artisan leaders with the choice of aspiring to bourgeois status or sinking into the growing numbers of itinerant journeymen and women who formed the basis of Lyon's proletariat. The weavers who had family workshops and several looms rejected proletarianization; it appeared to them that working for someone else in another's establishment was fitting for an apprentice or journeyman, not for a mature craftsman, certainly not for a husband and father. The artisans, therefore, did everything in their power to retain their elite position amongst the workers and to restore the world they had lost by creating cooperative associations.

None of these associations admitted the growing number of women weavers who were employed in factories. The only women in the associations were wives of weavers who performed traditional preparatory work for placing the silk on the loom. They continued to reaffirm the advice given to working women by a bourgeois lady in 1848: "My dear women, the wages of women are of little importance. The man is the head of the family, and when he earns well, the women are happy."[5]

To the questions posed by women workers:

> *And when he is sick or ill-tempered?*
> *And when the women are widows?*
> *And when they don't find husbands?*

They had no answers.

111

APPENDIX A

A Weaver's Balance Sheet

The first loom was set-up five different times during the year to weave the following products:

1. From May 1 to October 15 fabric for satin collars was woven; 143 meters @ 2fr51 cent. Total = 358 fr95.

2. From November 5 to January 10 coarse fabric for undergarments was woven; 200 meters @ 1fr10. Total = 220fr.

3. From January 25 to March 1 fabric for cashmere vests was made; 48 meters @ 2fr25. Total = 117fr60.

4. From April 15 to April 25 novelty vest material was woven; 100 meters @ 1fr. Total = 100fr.

5. The fifth setting up of the loom produced nothing. The costs for setting-up were paid by the fabricant. Total = 32fr.

The total revenue from the first loom for the year was 828fr55.

The second loom was set-up five times:

1. From August 10 to August 15 fabric for dresses was woven; 212 meters @ 1fr15. Total = 243fr80.

2. From September 1 to October 15 fabric for silk ties was made; 75 meters @ 1fr50. Total = 112fr50.

3. From November 10 to January 10 fabric for making silk buttons was woven; 130 meters @ 1fr25. Total = 162fr50.

4. From January 20 to March 20 novelty fabric for silk vests were woven; 150 meters @ 1fr50. Total = 225fr.

5. From 25 March to May 1 fabric for ties was woven; 75 meters @ 1fr. Total = 75fr.

The total revenue from the second loom was 818fr80.

The third loom was set-up four times during the year:

1. From May 5 to September 10 it was used for mixed silk and cotton or wool to make vests; 420 meters @ 75 centimes. Total = 315fr.

2. From September 15 to November 25 fabric for cashmere collars was woven; 55 meters @ 2fr50. Total = 137fr50.

3. From December 1 to January 15 fabric for cashmere vests was woven; 30 meters @ 2fr70. Total = 81fr.

4. From February 1 to May 10 fabric for furniture upholstry was woven; 200 meters @ 2fr. Total = 400fr.

The total revenue from the third loom was 933fr50.

The fourth loom was set-up five times.

1. From May 12 to July 5 it was used to weave fabric for richly decorated collars; 36 meters @ 4fr50. Total = 162fr.

2. From July 10 to November 1 cashmere for collars was woven; 170 meters @ 2fr70. Total = 459fr.

3. From December 1 to February 7 coarse silk was woven for vests; 180 meters @ 1fr10. Total = 198fr.

113

4. From March 4 to April 10 mixed fabric for vests was woven; 50 meters @ 80 centimes. Total = 40fr.

5. From April 15 to May 5 ties were woven; 75 meters at 65 centimes. Total = 48fr75.

The total revenue from the fourth loom was 907fr75. The total income from all four looms came to 3,488fr60. To this sum we must add 45fr which the fabricants advanced to pay for silk materials and 13fr30 which he advanced for cotton and woolen materials. The total revenue was thus 3,546fr90.

Total Expenses:	Setting up, replacing parts on the loom, feeding workers who prepared looms for new job	= 600fr
	Reelers and twisters	= 294fr
	Payment for three compagnons	= 2,229fr

1,318fr was left for personal use of chef and family:

	Estimated annual cost of clothing	= 100fr
	Housekeeping	= 40fr
	Food for three (3fr per day)	= 1,095fr
	Laundry	= 40fr
	Shoes	= 25fr
	Coal	= 45fr
	Rent	= 250fr

Total   = 1,595fr

Annual deficit for chef   = 277

From, "Letter to the Editor", *L'Echo de l'Industrie*, March 14, 1846.

APPENDIX B

Chart 1

	Number of Silk Workers	Number of Unskilled Workers
Sex-Related Arrests	14	49
Non-Sex Arrests	41	88

Chart 2

	Address	No Address
Sex-Related Arrests	35	48
Non-Sex Arrests	151	71

Chart 3

	No Data	15 and under	16-20	21-25	26-30	31-35	36-40	41-45	46-50	51-55	56-over
Sex Related Arrests	1	2	8	45	18	0	5	2	1	0	1
Non-Sex Arrests	7	7	21	56	34	17	19	9	20	6	26

117

APPENDIX C

L'Apostolat des Femmes — Women's Mission

Le Censeur — The Censor

Le Conseiller des Femmes — The Women's Advisor

Le Courrier de Lyon — The Courrier

L'Echo de la Fabrique — The Silk Workers' Voice

L'Echo des Travailleurs — The Workers' Voice

La Femme de L'Avenir — The Woman of the Future

La Femme Libre — The Free Woman

La Femme Nouvelle — The New Woman

Le Journal des Femmes — The Women's Journal

La Mère de Famille — The Mother of the Family

Mosaique Lyonnaise — Lyonese Mosaic

Le Papillon — The Butterfly

La Tribune des Femmes — The Tribune of Women

BIBLIOGRAPHY

A. Archives

ARCHIVES NATIONALES

BB [18] - Rapports des Procureurs Généraux et des Procureurs du Roi au Garde des Sceaux, Ministre de la Justice. Consulted:

1426	9329		
1452	3825	2869	
1455	4304	4493	
1458	4604	4698	4969
1463	5756		

BB [24] Ministre de la Justice: Direction des Affaires Criminelles et des Graces.
327-47   S-37181

BB [30] Division Criminelle
299 - 1-1799
300   2951
301
302
327 (1) Mission de Jouve de Bor
361(3)
C   943-969 - L'Enquête sur la condition ouvrière de 1848.

F [7] - Police
12239 - Individus en surveillance
12243 - Infanticide
4145   Police de Rhône 1834-41
4146   Police de Rhône 1842-55 (48-55 mostly missing)

F¹¹   Produits des Récoltes

F¹²   Commerce et Industrie
       2390   Filature de Soie
       2419   Dévidage des Fils
       2199   Métiers Jacquard - soie (1811-66)
       2413   Tissage des Etoffes (1765-1845)

ARCHIVES MUNICIPALES DE LYON

R¹ & R² Ecoles

I^e Emeute

I² 40. Troubles politiques

Actes de mariage, Croix-Rousse

Recensement de la population, Croix-Rousse: 1831-51

Naissance, 1827

ARCHIVES DEPARTEMENTALES DU RHÔNE

V/52   Publication du reglement pour les oblations.

ARCHIVES DE L'ARCHEVEQUE DE LYON

Sacra Rituum Congregatio, Sectio Historica, no. 143
Lettres du Mgr le Cardinal de Bonald
Lyon et ses oeuvres, 1960
Manuel des Oeuvres de Lyon, 1926 and 1976

B. Contemporary Journals

LYON:

Le Censeur

La Commune Sociale (1848-49).

Le Conseiller des Femmes (Nov. 1833-Sept. 1834).

Le Courrier de Lyon

L'Echo de la Fabrique (1842-45).

L'Echo de l'Industrie: Journal des intérêts des travailleurs et de la fabrique lyonnaise (1845-56).

L'Egalité (Aug. 1849).

Journal du Commerce de la Ville de Lyon et du Département du Rhône (1835-44).

La Liberté: Journal de Lyon (1848).

La Montagne St-Just et la Croix-Rousse (1848, 2 issues).

Le Mosaique Lyonnaise: Journal Littéraire, arts, sciences, industrie, nouvelle, théâtres, modes. (Oct. 1834-Jan. 1835).

Le Papillon: Journal des dames, des salons, des arts, de la littérature, des théâtres, et des modes. (Appeared bi-weekly: July 1832-1833 and July-October 1834).

Le Peuple Souverain: Journal de Lyon (1848-1849).

Le Tribun des peuple (Lyon 1848).

La Voix du peuple (Lyon 1848).

Les Travailleurs (1849-1850).

121

La Tribune Lyonnaise: Revue politique, sociale, industrielle, scientifique et littéraire des travailleurs (May 1845-1851).

PARIS:

L'Atelier (1840-1850).

La Democratie Pacifique

La Femme Libre (1832-1834). Name changed as follows: *La Femme Nouvelle, Femme d'Avenir, Apostolat des Femmes, Tribune des Femmes.*

Le Journal des Femmes (1832-1838).

La Mère de Famille (1833-?).

L'Opinion des Femmes (1848-1849).

La Politique des Femmes (1848).

C. Other Published Sources

Abensour, Leon, *La Femme et le féminisme avant la révolution,* Paris: Leroux, 1923.

Abensour, Leon, "Le Féminisme pendant le règne de Louis-Philippe," *La Révolution Francaise,* vol. 55, 1908.

Abensour, Leon, "Le Feminisme sous la monarchie de juillet," *La Révolution Francaise,* vol. 56, 1909.

Abensour, Leon, "Le Féminisme sous la monarchie de juillet: Les essais de réalisation et les résultats," *Revue D'Histoire Moderne et Contemporaine,* vol. 15, 1911.

Aboucaya, Claude, *Les Structures sociales et economiques de l'agglomeration lyonnaise à la veille de la Révolution de 1848,* Paris: 1963.

Affiches de la Societe La Voix des Femmes, 9th session, June 6, 1848.

Affiche du Club des Femmes, 1st session, June 12, 1848.

Aguet, Jean-Pierre, *Les Grèves sous la monarchie de juillet 1830-1847*, Geneva: Librairie E. Droz, 1954.

Alazard, "La Population ouvrière sous la monarchie de juillet," *La Revue de Mois*, 1911.

Alcan, Michel, *Essai sur l'industrie des matières textiles comprenant le travail complet du coton, du lin, des laines, du cachemire, etc.*, Paris: 1847.

Allart, Mme. Hortense, *La Femme de la démocratie de nos temps*, Paris: 1836.

Anderson, R.D., *Education in France 1848-1870*, London: 1975.

Antoine de St.-Gervais, A., *Le Moraliste du jeune age*, Rouen, 1835.

Ariès, Philippe, "Interpretation pour une histoire des mentalités," in Helen Bergues, ed., *La Prevention des Naissances dans la famille, ses origines dans le temps modernes*, Paris: 1960.

Arminjou, V., *La Population du département du Rhône, son évolution depuis le début du XIXe siecle*, Lyon: Bosc Frères, 1940.

Arnaud, Mme. Angelique, "Les disciples de St-Simon," *Droit des Femmes*, 1870.

Arnaune, Alphonse, *Le Commerce exterieur et les tarifs de douanes*, Paris: 1911.

Amé, Leon, *Etude sur les tarifs de douanes et sur les traités de commerce*, 2 vols., 3rd edition, Paris:

Annuaire départemental du Rhône, 1842.

Ashley, Percy, *Modern Tariff History*, London: 1920.

Association des dames du Calvaire, en faveur des pauvres femmes incurables délaissées, 15 Dec. 1843, Lyon: 1843.

Association fraternelle des femmes ouvrières lyonnaises pour l'exploitation des toutes les industries, Lyon: 1848.

Audiganne, Armand, *Les Populations ouvrières et les industries de la France dans le mouvement social du XIXe siecle*, 2 vols., Paris: Capelle, 1854.

Augier, *Le Canut*, n.d.

L'Avenir des Travailleurs (June 1848, 2 issues).

Ballot, Charles, *L'Introduction du machinisme dans l'industrie française*, Paris: Rieden, 1923.

Bardèche, Maurice, *Histoire des femmes*, 2 vol. Paris: Stock, 1968.

Baudot, *La Situation de l'enseignement primaire dans le departement du Rhône*, Lyon, 1836.

Beaugé, Charles, "Dépenses et salaires de la class ouvrière en 1840," *Journal des Economistes*, 6 serie t. LXXVII, Jan.-Mar. 1924.

Beaulieu, Charles, *Histoire de commerce de l'industrie et des fabriques de Lyon*, Lyon: 1838.

Beauquis, A., *Histoire économique de la soie*, Paris: 1910.

Beaurieux, Noel, *Le prix du blé en France au XIX* e *siecle*, Paris: 1909.

Berger, Peter, *et al.*, *The Homeless Mind: Modernization and Consciousness*, N.Y., 1973.

Bez, Abbé N., *La Ville des aumônes, tableau des oeuvres de charité de la ville de Lyon*, Lyon, 1940.

Bez, Abbé N., *De l'etablissement religieux-industriel*, Lyon: 1846.

Bezucha, Robert J., *The Lyon Uprising of 1834*, Cambridge, 1974.

Blanqui, Aîné, *Rapport sur la situation des ouvriers en soie de Lyon*. Lyon: l'Academie des sciences morales et politiques, 1849.

Barsalou, Gustave, *Etudes sur le passé et sur l'avenir des travailleurs industriels*, Paris: 1848.

Bennet, Jean, *L'Admission des femmes dans les associations de prévoyance jusqu'a la fin du XIX* e *siecle*, Etampes: Societe Regionale D'Imprimerie et de Publicité, 1954.

Bère, Emile, *Des classes ouvrières: Moyens d'améliorer leur sort sous le rapport du bien-être materiel et du perfectionnement moral*, Paris: Charpentier, 1836.

Bertin, George, *L'Organisation du travail considérée sous le rapport de l'emploi de la femme dans l'industrie*, Nantes: 1848.

Blanc, Elénore, *Biographie de Flora Tristan*, Lyon: 1845.

Blanc, Louis, *Organisation du travail*, Paris: Pagnerre, 1840.

Blanqui, Adolphe, *Des Classes ouvrières en France pendant l'année 1848*, Paris: L'Academie des sciences morales et politiques, 1849.

Boas, Franz, "Education, Conformity, and Cultural Change," in Roberts and Akinoanyh, eds., *Educational Patterns and Cultural Configurations*, N.Y., 1976.

Bougeart, Alfred, *Tout ou rien, par un homme du peuple*, Paris: 1840.

Boullet, Bernard, *L'Organisation de l'orientation professionelle et de l'apprentissage*, Paris: Dunod, 1941.

Bourgin, Hubert, "L'Histoire économique de la France 1800-1830," *Revue d'Histoire Moderne et Contemporaine*, VI, 1905.

Bourgin, Hubert, "La Législation ouvrière du second empire," *Revue des ètudes napoléonienne*, IV, 1913.

Bouvery, Louis-Joseph, *Causes de la misère et moyens pour la détruire*, Lyon: 1848.

Boyer, Adolphe, *De l'Etat des ouvriers et de son amélioration par l'organisation du travail*, Paris: C. Dubois, 1841.

Bridel, Louis, *Hommes et femmes, droit français comparé*, Paris: L. Larose et Tenin, 1908.

Briquet, Jean, *Agricol Perdiguier: Compagnon du tour de France et réprésentant du peuple*, Paris: Marcel Rivière et cie, 1955.

Bruhat, Jean, *Histoire du mouvement ouvrier francais: Des Origines à la révolte des canuts*, Paris: Editions Sociales, 1952.

Buret, Eugène, *La misère des classes laborieuses en France et en Angleterre*, Paris: Paulin, 1840.

Burette, *Societé fraternelle de secours mutuels et d'organisation du travail, fondée à Lyon en Sept. 1848*, La Croix-Rousse: 1848.

Cabet, Etienne, "La Femme," *Douze lettres d'un communiste à un reformiste sur la communauté*, Paris: Bureau du Populaire, Oct. 1848.

Cabet, Etienne, *La Femme, son malheureux sort dans la societé actuelle son bonheur dans la communauté*, Paris: Delanchy, 1844.

Chaissaignon, *Devoir de liberté: Chansons de compagnons et autres*, Paris: 1836.

Chambre de Commerce de Lyon, *Rapport, projet de statuts et délibera-tion pour l'établissement à Lyon d'une caisse de secours et de retraites pour les employés de deux sexes de la fabrique de soie*, Lyon: 1849.

Charavay, Jean, *Projet d'association fraternelle de l'industrie française*, Lyon: 1848.

Charlety, Sebastien, *Bibiliographie critique de l'histoire de Lyon depuis 1789 jusqu'à nos jours*, 2 vols., Lyon: 1903.

Chevallier, Emile V., *Les Salaires au 19e siecle*, Paris: 1887.

Chevalier, Louis, *Classes laborieuses et classes dangereuses à Paris pendant la première moitié du XIXe siècle*, Paris: Plon, 1958.

Cochin, Augustin, *De la condition des ouvriers français d'après les derniers travaux*, Paris: Douniol, 1862.

Collombet, F.Z., "Les soeurs de Bon-Secours," *Revue de Lyonnaise*, I, x. 47, 1839.

Colls, Robert, " 'O Happy English Children!': Coal, Class and Educa-tion in the North East," *Past and Present*, vol. 73.

Colomes, André, *Les ouvriers du textile dans la Champagne troyenne, 1730-1852*, Paris: Domat Montchrestien, 1943.

Combes, Louis de, *Clubs revolutionnaires de lyonnaises*, Lyon: Trevoux, 1908.

Combet, Louis, *La Lyonnaise de 1847*, La Guillotiere: 1847.

Commissaire, Sebastien, *Memoires et souvenirs*, Lyon: Meton, 1888.

Comte, Auguste, *Plan des travaux nécessaires pour réorganiser la société*, Paris: 1822.

Compte rendu par l'administration du refuge St-Joseph, Lyon: 1847.

Condition des ouvriers de Paris de 1789 jusqu'en 1841, avec quelques idées sur la possibilité de l'ameliorer, Paris: J-B Gros, 1841.

Conseil General du Département du Rhône, *Rapports sur l'administration du département présenté par le préfet Lyon*, since 1836, 1 vol. per year.

Coornaert, Emile, *Les Compagnonnages en France du moyen age à nos jours*, Paris: Les Editions Ouvrières, 1966.

Coornaert, Emile, *Les Corporations en France avant 1789*, Paris: Gallimard, 1941.

Coornaert, Emile, "La Pensée ouvrière et la conscience de classe en France," *Studi in Onore di Gino Luzzato*, vol. III, Milano: Guiffre, 1950.

Coquelin, Charles, "De l'Industrie Linière en France et en Angleterre," *Revue des Deux Mondes*, series 4, 19, 1839.

Cuvillier, Armand, *Hommes et idéologies de 1840*, Paris: Rivière et Cie, 1956.

Cuvillier, Armand, *Un Journal des ouvriers: L'Atelier, 1840-1850*, Paris: Les Editions Ouvrières, 1954.

Czynski, Jean, *Avenir des ouvriers*, Paris: Librairie Sociale, 1839.

Daubie, J-V, *La Femme pauvre au XIXe siècle*, vol. I, conditions economique, Paris: 1870.

Daumas, Maurice, ed., *Histoire générale des techniques: L'Expansion du machinisme*, Paris: 1968.

Daussigny, *De l'Organisation du travail de la fabrication des étoffes de soie*, Lyon: Nigon, 1848.

Demar, Claire, *Ma Loi d'avenir*, Paris: 1834.

Deslandres, Maurice et Michelin, Alfred, *Il y a cent ans: Etat physique et moral des ouvriers au temps du liberalisme, témoignage de Villermé*, Paris: 1938.

Dolléans, Edouard, *Féminisme et mouvement ouvrier: George Sand*, Paris: Les Editions Ouvrières, 1951.

Dolléans, Edouard, *Histoire du mouvement ouvrier, 1830-1871*, vol. 1, fourth edition, Paris: Librairie Armand Colin, 1948.

Dolléans, Edouard, *Histoire du travail*, Paris: Domat-Montchrestien, 1943.

Droux, *La Chanson lyonnaise*, Lyon: 1907.

Dubuisson, Jane, "Institutions de bienfaisance: Refuge de St-Joseph à Oullins," *Revue de Lyonnaise*, vol. 10.

DuCellier, F., *Les classes ouvrières en France depuis 1789*, Paris: 1857.

DuCellier, F., *Histoire des classes laborieuses en France*, Paris: 1860.

Duchâtélet, Parent, *Prostitution dans la ville de Paris*, 2 volumes, Paris: J.B. Baillière, 1836.

Ducpetiaux, Edouard, *De la condition physique et morale des jeunes ouvriers*, 2 vols., Brussels: 1843.

Dunham, Arthur Louis, "Industrial Life and Labor in France, 1815-1848," *Journal of Economic History*, III, 1943.

Dunham, Arthur Louis, *The Industrial Revolution in France 1815-1848*, New York: Exposition Press, 1955.

Dunham, Arthur Louis, "The Economic History of France, 1815-1870," *Journal of Modern History*, 21, 1949.

Dupont-White, Charles, *Essai sur les relations du travail avec le capital*, Paris: 1846.

Dutacq, Francois, *Histoire politique de Lyon pendant la révolution de 1848*, Paris: E. Cornely et Cie, 1910.

Duveau, Georges, *La Vie ouvrière en France sous le second empire*, Paris: 1946.

Efrahem, *De l'Association des ouvriers de tous les corps d'état*, Paris: Auguste Mie, 1873.

Egron, A.C., *Le Livre de l'ouvrier, ses devoirs envers la société, la famille et lui-même*, Paris: 1844.

Elwitt, Sanford, *The Making of the Third Republic*, Baton Rouge, 1975.

English, W., *The Textile Industry: Silk Production and Manufacture, 1750-1900*, Oxford: Clarendon Press, 1958.

Espinas, Georges, "Une bibliographie de l'histoire économique et sociale moderne et contemporaine," *Nierteljahrschrift fur Sozialund Wirtschaftsageschichte*, III, 1905.

Favre, Jules, *De la Coalition des chefs d'atelier de Lyon*, Lyon: 1833.

Festy, Octave, "Le Mouvement ouvrier à Paris en 1840," *Revue des sciences politiques*, 30, 1913.

Festy, Octave, *Le Mouvement ouvrier au debut de la monarchie de juillet 1830-1834*, Paris: E. Cornely, 1908.

Fleury, Abbé, *Petit catechism historiques*, Lyon: 1816.

Fixe, Theodore, *Observations sur l'état des classes ouvrières*, Paris: Guillaumin, 1845.

Fouin, L-F, *De l'Etat des domestiques en France et des moyens propres à les moraliser*, Paris: Delauney, 1837.

Fourier, Charles, *Le nouveau monde industriel et societaire*, Paris: Bossangé père, 1829.

Fourier, Charles, *Traite de l'Association domestique et agricole*, 2 vols., Paris: 1822 and 1840.

Fournière, Eugène, *Le Règne de Louis-Philippe*, Paris: 1906.

Fournière, Eugène, *Les théories socialistes au XIXe siècle*, de Babeuf à Proudhon, Paris: Alcan, 1909.

France, Bureau de Statistique Générale, *Statisque générale*, Paris: 1835-1873.

France, Ministère du Travail, *Salaires et cout de l'existence à diverses époques jusqu'en 1910*, Paris: 1911.

France, Office du Travail, *Salaires et durée du travail dans l'industrie française*, 5 vols., Paris: 1893-1897.

Fregier, Honoré Antoine, *Des classes dangereuses de la population dans les grandes villes, et des moyens de les rendres meilleures*, 2 vols., Paris: 1840.

Gaillard, Léon et Neulat, L., *Les Droits de la Femme devant la loi française*, Paris: Librairie mondiale, 1907.

Garden, Maurice, *Lyon et les lyonais an XVIIIe siècle*, Paris: 1970.

Gaumont, Jean, *Le développement de la coopération ouvrière dans la banlieue parisienne*, Paris: Presses Universitaires de France, 1933.

Gaumont, Jean, *Le Mouvement ouvrier d'association et de coopération à Lyon*, Lyon: Avenir regionale, 1921.

Gide, Paul, *Etude sur la condition privée de la femme*, Paris: Durand et Pedone-Laurier, 1867.

Gille, Bertrand, *Les Sources statistiques de l'histoire de France, des enquêtes du XVII^{e}siècle à 1870*, Geneva: Droz, 1964.

Gille, Bertrand, *Récherches sur la formation de la grande enterprise capitaliste 1815-1848*, Paris: S.E.V.P.E.N., 1959.

Godechot, Jacques, ed., *La Presse ouvrière 1819-1850*, Paris: Presses Universitaires, 1968.

Goldsmith, Margaret Leland, *Seven Women against the World*, London: Methuen and Co. Ltd., 1935.

Gosset, *Projet tendant à régénerer le compagnonnage sur le tour de France, soumis à tous les ouvriers*, Paris: 1842.

Grandin, A., *Bibliographie générale des sciences juridiques, politiques, économiques, et sociales de 1800 à 1925-1926*, 4 vols., Paris: 1926.

Grignon, *Réflexions d'un ouvrier tailleur sur la misère des ouvriers en général*, Paris: 1833.

Gueneau, Louis, *Lyon et le commerce de la soie*, Lyon: Bascon, 1923.

Guilbaud, P.A., *Plan pour l'établissement comme germe d'harmonie societaire d'une maison rurale industrielle d'apprentissage pour 200 elèves de toutes classes, garçons et filles de 5 à 13 ans*, Paris: 1839.

Guillaumon, *Confessions d'un compagnon*, Paris: 1858.

Guinot, Jean-Pierre, *Formation professionelle et travailleurs qualifiés depuis 1789*, Paris: Demot-Montchrestien, 19?.

Hafter, Daryl M., "Philippe de Lasalle: From Mise-en-Carte to Industrial Design," *Winterthur Portfolio*, vol. XII, 1977.

Hedde, Philippe, "Aperçu sur l'état actual des fabriques de rubans de St-Etienne et de St-Chamond en 1828," *Société Industrielle de St-Etienne*, Bulletin 6, 1828.

Hunt, H.J., *Le socialisme et le romantisme en France: Etude de la presse socialiste de 1830 à 1840*, Oxford: Clarendon Press, 1935.

Imbert, *Des Crèches et de l'allaitement maternal*, Lyon: 1847.

Isambert, Gaston, *Les Idées socialistes en France de 1815 à 1848*, Paris: 1905.

Jaume, A., *Histoire des classes laborieuses, precédée d'un essai sur l'economie industrielle et sociale*, Toulon: E. Aurel, 1852.

Jefferson, Carter, "Worker Education in England and France," *Comparative Studies in Society and History*, vol. 6.

Labrousse, C.-Ernest, *Le Mouvement ouvrier et les idées sociales en France de 1815 à la fin du XIX e siècle*, Paris: Centre de documentation universitaire.

Lasch, Christopher, "Family and History," *New York Review of Books*, Dec. 1975.

Lavigne, Pierre, *Le Travail dans les constitutions françaises 1789-1945*, Paris: Librairie du Recueil Sirey, 1948.

Lebey, André, "Liste de Quelque Clubs de Lyon d'après des medialles," *Révolution de 1848 et les révolutions du XIX e siécle*, #6.

Leon, Pierre, "La Region lyonnaise dans l'histoire economique et sociale de la France," *Revue Historique*, CCXXXVII.

Lequin, Yves, *Les Ouvriers de la région lyonnaise, 1848-1914*, Lyon: 1977.

Leroux, Jules, *Aux Ouvriers typographs: de la Nécessité de fonder une association ayant pour but de rendre les ouvriers propriétaires de leurs instruments de travail,* Paris: Hernan, 1833.

Leroy-Beaulieu, Paul, "Les Ouvrières de fabrique autrefois et aujourd'hui," *Revue des deux mondes,* XCVII, 1872.

LeSenne, *Droits et devoirs de la femme devant la loi française,* 2nd ed., Paris: A. Henneye, 1902.

Levasseur, Ernest, *Histoire des classes ouvrières et de l'industrie en France,* 2 vols., 2nd ed., Paris: Arthur Rousseau, 1903.

Levy, Claude, "La Fabrique de soie lyonnaise 1830-1848," *1848 et les révolutions du XIXe siècles,* été, t.37, #177, 1947.

Levy-Schneider, "Les Debuts de la revolution de 1848 à Lyon," *Revue d'Histoire Moderne,* tome XV, 1911.

Lichtheim, George, *The Origins of Socialism,* Boston, Praeger, 1969.

Le Livret c'est le servage, Paris: La Democratie Pacifique, 1847.

Louis, Paul, *Histoire de la classe ouvrière en France de la Révolution à nos jours,* Paris: Riviere, 1927.

Lyon, L.J., *La Lyre du Devoir* (song), 1846.

McKay, D.C., *The National Workshops,* Cambridge: 1933.

Mada, A., *Le Droit des femmes au travail,* Paris: 1904.

Malepeyre, Leopold, *Code des ouvriers ou recueil methodique des lois et règlements concernant les ouvriers, chefs d'ateliers, contre-maitres, compagnons et apprentis, avec des notes explicatives,* Paris: Société Nationale, 1833.

Maritch, Sreten, *Histoire du mouvement social à Lyon sous le Second Empire,* Paris: 1930.

Marseillaise des Compagnons (song), 1848.

Martin, Germain, *Histoire economique et financière de la France,* Paris: 1927.

Martin-St-Leon, Etienne, *Le Compagnonnage, son histoire, ses coutumes, ses règlements et ses rites,* Paris: Armand Colin, 1901.

Martin-St-Leon, Etienne, *Histoire des corporations de metiers,* Paris: Guillaumin, 1897.

Mazaroz, Paul, *Etudes sur l'ouvrier des ville,* Paris: Lacroix, 1862.

Mazoyer, Louis, "Catégories d'âges et groupes sociaux: les Jeunes générations françaises de 1830," *Annales d'histoire economique et sociale,* Sept. 1938.

Mazoyer, Louis, "L'Ouvrier de 1830 et sa vision du monde social," *Revue Socialiste,* Nov., 1946, Jan. 1947.

Merson, Ernest, *De la Situation des classes ouvrières en France,* Paris, Guillaumin, 1849.

Michel, Andrée, "Interaction and Family Planning in the French Urban Family," *Demography,* Vol. IV.

Milhaud, Carolyne, *L'Ouvrière en France,* Paris: 1907.

Mittre, Marius-Henri-Casimir, *Des Domestiques en France dans leurs rapports avec l'économie sociale, le bonheur domestique, les lois civiles, criminelles et de police,* Paris: Mittre, 1837.

Michelet, Jules, *La Femme,* Paris: Hachette, 1860.

Monfalcon, J.B. and Polinière, A.P.I., *Conseil d'hygiene et de salubrité du département du Rhône,* Lyon: Nigon, 1851.

Monfalcon, J.B., *Histoire monumental,* vol. 3, Lyon: 18?

Monfalcon, J.B., and Polinière, A.P.I., *Salubrité des grandes villes,* Lyon: 18?

Morazé, Charles, *La France bourgeoise,* Paris: Armand Colin, 1946.

Moreau, Pierre, *Un Mot sur le compagnonnage ou le guide de l'ouvrier sur le Tour de France,* Paris: 1841.

Moreau, Pierre, *Un Mot aux ouvriers de toutes les professions ou le guide de l'ouvrier sur le Tour de France,* Auxerre: Guillaume Maillefer, 1841.

Moreau, Pierre, *De la Reforme des abus du compagnonnage,* Paris: Prevost, 1843.

Moreau de Jonnes, Alexandre, "*Travail et salaires agricoles en France,*" Journal des Economistes, XXVII, 1850.

Notice historique sur la fondation de la Société de l'Union des travailleurs du Tour de France, 3 e édition, Tours: 1900.

Perdiguier, Agricole, *Le Livre du compagnonnage,* Paris: 1840.

Paillat, Paul, "*Les Salaires et la condition ouvrière en France à l'aube du machinisme,*" Revue économique, 1951.

Pariset, Ernest, *Histoire de la fabrique lyonaise: étude sur la regime social et économique de l'industrie de la soie à Lyon, depuis le XVI e siècle,* Lyon: A. Rey, 1901.

Pariset, Ernest, *Les Industries de la soie: sericiculture, filature, moulinage, tissage, teinture, histoire et statistiques,* Lyon: Pitrat Aîné, 1890.

Peigné, Louis, *La Recitation à l'école primaire,* Paris: 2nd ed., 1916.

Perdiguier, Agricole, *Memoires d'un compagnon,* Paris: Union Générales d'Editions, 1964.

Perennes, Francois, *De la Domesticité avant et depuis 1789,* Paris: Sagnier et Bray, Sept. 1844.

Perruchot, Henri, "Flora Tristan, Grand-mère de Gauguin," *Les Oeuvres Libres,* Paris: Librairie Artheme Fayard, 26 Sept. 1961.

Pinchbeck, Ivy, *Women Workers and the Industrial Revolution 1750-1850,* London: Geo. Routledge & Sons, Ltd., 1930.

Portal, Magda, *Flora Tristan, la precursora,* Lima: Paginas libres, 1945.

Potton, A., *De la Prostitution et de ses conséquences dans les grandes villes, dans la ville de Lyon en particulier,* Lyon et Paris: 1842.

Pouthas, *La Population française pendant la première moitié du XIX siècle,* Paris: Presses Universitaires de France, 1956.

Projets d'association libre et volontaire entre les chefs d'industrie et les ouvriers, et de reforme commerciale, adoptés et publiés par le comité de l'organisation du travail de Lyon, Lyon: 1848.

Puech, Jules-L., "Flora Tristan et le Perou," *Revue de l'Amerique latine,* Paris: 1925.

Puech, Jules-L., *Le Socialisme avant 1848: La Vie et l'oeuvre de Flora Tristan (1803-1844),* Paris: Riviere, 1925.

Quentin-Bauchart, Pierre, *La Crise Sociale de 1848,* Paris: 1920.

Ragon, Michel, *Histoire de la littérature ouvrière,* Paris: Editions Ouvrières, 1953.

Règlement du Mont de Piété de Lyon, Lyon: 1836.

Reveil, E., "Associations fraternelles et politiques à Lyon (1848-1850)," *Revue D'Histoire de Lyon,* vol. IV, 1905.

Reybaud, Louis, *Etudes sur le regime des manufactures: La Condition des ouvriers en soie,* Paris: Michel-Levy frères, 1859.

Reybaud, Louis, *La Vie de l'employé,* Crete: Corbeil, 1854.

Reynier, Joseph, *Memoires d'un ancien tisseur,* Lyon: 1898.

Rigaudas-Weiss, Hilde, *Les Enquêtes ouvrières en France entre 1838 et 1848,* Paris: Alcan, 1936.

Rist, Charles, "La durée du travail dans l'industrie française de 1820 à 1870," *Revue d'économie politique,* III, 1897.

Rodrigues, Olinde, ed., *Oeuvres de Saint-Simon,* Paris: Capelle, 1871.

Rodrigues, Olinde, ed., *Poésie sociale des ouvriers,* Paris: Paulin, 1941.

Rondot, Natalis, *La fabrique lyonnaise de soieries et l'industrie de la soie en France, 1789-1889,* Lyon: 1889.

Rowbotham, Sheila, *Women, Resistance, and Revolution,* N.Y., 1972.

Rude, Fernand, *Le Mouvement ouvrier à Lyon de 1827-1832,* Paris: Domat-Montchrestien, 1944.

Sée, Henri, "Esquisse de l'évolution industrielle de la France de 1815 à 1848: La progrès du machinisme et de la concentration," *Revue d'Histoire économique et sociale*, 1923.

Sée, Henri, *Histoire économique de la France 1789-1914*, Paris: Librairie Armand Colin, 1942.

Sée, Henri, "Recent Work in French Economic History," *Economic History Review*, I (1927).

Simon, Jules, L'Ouvrière, *Paris: 1861.*

Société d'union fraternelle et philanthropique des ouvriers tisseurs, Paris: Demouville, 1833.

Sullerot, Evelyne, *Histoire et sociologie du travail féminin*, Paris: Gonthiers, 1968.

Sullerot, Evelyne, *La Presse Féminine*, Paris: Armand-Colin, 1963.

Statuts de l'institution des salles d'asiles catholiques de Lyon, Lyon: 1840.

Tarle, Eugene, "La Grande coalition des mineurs de Rive de Gier en 1844," *Revue Historique*, CLXXVII, 1936.

Tchernoff, Iouda, *Le Parti Republicain sous la Monarchie de Juillet*, Paris: 1901.

Thibert, Marguerite, *La Féminisme dans le socialisme français 1830-1850*, Paris: Giard, 1926.

Thierrat, Philippe, *Du Malaise de la classe ouvrière et de l'institution des Prud'hommes, appliquée à l'organisation du travail dans la fabrique lyonnaise*, Lyon: 1848.

Thomas, Edith, *Les Femmes de 1848*, Paris: 1948.

Thomas, Edith, *George Sand*, Paris: Editions Universitaires, 1959.

Thomas, Edith, *Pauline Roland: Socialisme et féminisme au XIX siècle*, Paris: Riviere, 1956.

Thomas, Keith, "Work and Leisure in Pre-Industrial Society," *Past and Present*, Dec. 1964.

Thompson, E.P., *The Making of the English Working Class*, New York: Vintage, 1963.

Thompson, E.P., "Time, Work-Discipline, and Industrial Capitalism," *Past and Present*, Dec. 1967.

Thouvenin, Dr., "De l'Influence que l'industrie exerce sur la santé des populations dans les grand centres manufacturiers," *Annales d'hygiène publique et de medicine legale*, serie 1, 36, 1846, and 37, 1847.

Tixerant, Jules, *Le Féminisme à l'époch de 1848 dans l'ordre politique et dans l'ordre économique*, Paris: Giard & Briere, 1908.

Tristan, Flora, *L'Emancipation de la femme; ou le testament de la paria,* posthumous work edited by A. Constant, Paris: Au bureau de la direction de la Verité, 1846.

Tristan, Flora, *Nécéssité de faire un bon accueil aux femmes étrangères,* Paris: Mme. Huzard, 1836.

Tristan, Flora, *Pérégrinations d'une paria,* Paris: Arthur Bertrand, 1838.

Tristan, Flora, *Pétition pour l'abolition de le peine de mort,* Paris: 19 Dec. 1838.

Tristan, Flora, *Pétition pour l'abolition de la peine de mort,* Paris: 19 Dec. 1837.

Tristan, Flora, *Promenades dans Londres,* Paris: H-L Dolloye, 1840.

Tristan, Flora, *Le Tour de France: journal inédit, 1843-1844,* Paris: 1973.

Tristan, Flora, *L'Union Ouvrière,* Paris: Prevot, 1843.

Tristan, Flora, *La Ville Monstre,* Paris: Delloye, 1842.

Truchon, Pierre, "La Vie Ouvrière sous la restauration," *Revue d'histoire de Lyon,* xi, 1912.

Truquin, Norbert, *Memoires et aventures d'un proletaire,* Paris: 1888.

Varnay, *La Verité au sujet du malaise de la fabrique,* Lyon: 1849.

Vermorel, J., *Quelques petits théâtres lyonnais des XVIII e et XIX e siècles,* Lyon: 1918.

Les Vésuviennes ou la constitution politique des femmes, par une société de françaises, avec l'épigraphe, "Pour tous et pour toutes," Flora Tristan, Paris: Baudruche, 1848.

Villermé, Dr. Louis, *Tableau de l'état physique et moral des ouvriers employés dans les manufactures de coton, de laine, et de soie,* Paris: Renouard, 1840.

Villiers, Marc de, *Histoire des clubs de femmes et des légions d'amazones,* Paris: Plon-Nourrit, 1910.

Vinçard, P., *Histoire du travail et des travailleurs en France,* 2 vols., Paris: 1845.

Vinçard, Jules, *Memoires épisodiques d'un vieux chansonnier saint-simonian,* Paris: 1848.

Voilquin, Suzanne, *Fille du Peuple,* Paris, 184?

La Voix des femmes: Journal socialiste et politique organe des intérêts de toutes (1848-?).

Weill, Georges, *L'Ecole St-Simonian,* Paris: Alcan, 1896.

Weill, Georges, *La France sous la Monarchie Constitutionelle (1814-1848),* Paris: Librairie Felix Alcan, 1912.

Weill, Georges, "Les Journaux ouvriers à Paris, 1830-1870," *Revue d'histoire moderne et contemporaine,* 1907.

Wells, Robert, "Family History and Demographic Transition," *Journal of Social History,* Fall 1975.

Wollstonecraft, Mary, *A Vindication of the Rights of Women,* N.Y.: 1967.

Zevaes, Alexandre, "Flora Tristan et l'Union Ouvrière," *Bibliothèque de la révolution de 1848,* 1935.

NOTES

Preface

[1] E.P. Thompson, *The Making of the English Working Class,* (New York, Vintage, 1963), p. 9.

NOTES

Chapter I

[1] Joseph Arminjou, *La Population du Département du Rhône: son évolution depuis le début du XIXe siècle,* Lyon: BOSC frères, 1940, pp. 23 and 29. The Rhône valley experienced a growth rate of 115%, while the French average growth for this period was only 50%. cf. Pouthas, *La Population Française pendant la première moitié du XIXe siècle,* Paris: Presses Universitaires de la France, 1956, p. 101.

[2] Pouthas, *op. cit.,* p. 101. The Croix-Rousse suburb was annexed to the city of Lyon in 1851.

[3] Arminjou, *op. cit.,* p. 34.

[4] Alexandre Moreau de Jonnès, *Statistique de L'Industrie de la France,* Paris: Guillaumin and Cie., 1856, pp. 153-4.

[5] Ernest Pariset, *Histoire de la Fabrique Lyonnaise,* Lyon: A. Rey, 1901.

[6] Ernest Pariset, *Les Industries de la Soie,* Lyon: Pitrat Aîné, 1890.

[7] *L'Echo de la fabrique,* #77, November 15, 1844.

[8] Pariset, *Histoire, op. cit.,* p. 306.

[9] "Report of the Prefect of the Rhône to Conseil General, 1844-45," *L'Echo de la fabrique,* #77.

[10] Dupont-White, *Essai sur les relations du travail avec le capital,* Paris: 1846, pp. 149, 152.

[11] Alazard, "La Population ouvrière sous la monarchie de juillet," *La Revue de Mois,* 1911, p. 586.

[12] McKay, D.C., *The National Workshops,* Cambridge, 1933, introduction.

13 Audiganne, Armand, *Les Populations ouvrières et les industries de la France dans le mouvement social du XIXe siècle*, Paris: Capelle, 1854, p. 229.

14 *L'Echo de la fabrique*, #17, November 15, 1844.

15 Pariset, *Histoire, op. cit.*, p. 306.

16 *Ibid.*, p. 306.

17 Levy-Schneider, "Les Débuts de la Révolution de 1848 à Lyon," *Revue d'Histoire Moderne*, 1911, t.xv, p. 36.

18 Pierre Quentin-Bauchart, *La Crise Sociale de 1848*, Paris: 1920, p. 129.

19 *Ibid.*, p. 83.

20 *L'Echo de l'industrie*, #14, Jan. 17, 1846.

21 Quentin-Bauchart, *op. cit.*, p. 128.

22 *Ibid.*, p. 129.

23 *L'Echo de la fabrique*, #33, Jan. 15, 1843.

24 Robert Bezucha, *The Lyon Uprising of 1834*, Cambridge: Harvard University Press, 1874, p. 23; cf. *L'Echo de l'industrie*, #13, Jan. 10, 1846.

25 Pariset, *Histoire, op. cit.*, p. 306.

26 "Report of the Tribunal of Commerce," *Echo de la fabrique*, #57, Jan. 15, 1844.

27 *Echo de la fabrique*, April 1844-January 1845.

28 Claude Aboucaya, *Les Structures sociales et economiques de l'agglomération lyonnaise à la veille de la Revolution de 1848*, Paris: 1963, p. 17; cf. *Tribune Lyonnaise*, March 1847, p. 6.

29 AN BB ¹⁸ 1420 8133. Letter dated Lyon, March 21, 1844.

30 *La Tribune Lyonnaise*, March 1, 1847.

31 "Revue de la fabrique," *Tribune Lyonnaise*, March 15, 1847, p. 6.

32 *Ibid.*, p. 6.

33 Arthur Dunham, *The Industrial Revolution in France*, New York: The Exposition Press, 1955, p. 325.

34 "Revue de la fabrique," *op. cit.*, p. 6.

35 Audiganne, *op. cit.*, p. 229.

36 "De la situation des tisseurs," *L'Echo de l'industrie*, #12, Jan. 3, 1846.

37 *L'Echo de la fabrique*, #72, Aug. 31, 1844. Flats were advertised as follows: "with or without rooms, cellars or gardens."

38 *L'Echo de l'industrie*, #5, Nov. 15, 1845.

39 "Revue de la fabrique," *op. cit.*, p. 6.

40 *L'Echo de la fabrique,* July 31, 1843. In one case brought before the Council, Mme. Verne, a weaver, told the court that her husband could not be present because he was forced to work as a coal miner, earning more money that way than by weaving. *Ibid.,* July 15, 1843.

41 *L'Echo de la fabrique,* #70, July 31, 1844. In the accounts of St-Joseph we find substantial contributions from merchants, and in a letter of 1837, Claudine Thévenet described the convent-workshop as a principal resource at Fourvière. *Compte rendu . . . St. Joseph,* Lyon: 1847. Archives de l'archevêché de Lyon, *Mariae a Sancto Ignatio* (Claudine Thévenet), Vatican City, 1967. Letter dated 1824.

42 Louis Reybaud, *Etudes sur le régime des manufactures: La condition des ouvriers en soie,* Paris: 1859, Appendix E.

43 *La Tribune Lyonnaise,* II, #7, September 1846, and III, #5, July 1847, p. 44.

44 *L'Echo de la fabrique,* #70, July 31, 1844.

45 *L'Echo de l'industrie,* #17, February 7, 1846.

46 *L'Echo de la fabrique,* #69, July 15, 1844.

47 *L'Echo de l'industrie,* March 14, 1846, all of the following information comes from a balance sheet in a letter to the editor (see Appendix A).

48 Bezucha, *op. cit.,* pp. 48-72, 149-174.

49 *L'Echo de l'industrie,* #14, January 17, 1846.

50 Archives Departementales, M32 2 *Caisse des Prêts,* cited in Claude Levy, "La Fabrique de soie Lyonnaise 1830-1848," *1848 et les révolutions du XIX e siècles,* été 1947, t.37, #177, p. 27. cf. "Enquête: Situation des ouvriers en soie à Lyon," *L'Atelier,* II, #9, May 1842, p. 69.

51 AD *Caisse des Prêts, op. cit.*

52 *Ibid.*

53 Annuaire departemental du Rhône, 1842, p. 7.

54 Tristan, *Journal, op. cit.,* May 22, 1844. cf. Monfalcon and Polinière, *Salubrité des Grandes Villes,* p. 437.

55 *L'Echo de la fabrique,* #33, Jan. 15, 1843.

56 Tristan, *Journal, op. cit.,* July 3, 1844.

57 *Ibid.,* p. 215.

NOTES

Chapter II

[1] Carolyne Milhaud, *L'Ouvrière en France*, Paris: 1907, p. 79.

[2] Dr. Louis Villermé, *Tableau de l'état physique et moral des ouvriers employés dans les manufactures de coton, de laine, et de soie*, Paris: Renouard, 1840, Vol. I, pp. 344-345.

[3] Ernest Pariset, *Les Industries de la Soie*, Lyon: Pitrat Aîné, 1890, p. 87.

[4] Dr. Thouvenin, "De l'Influence que l'industrie exerce sur la santé des populations dans les grand centres manufacturiers," *Annales d'Hygiène publique et de médécine légale*, Vol. 36, p. 36.

[5] Ernest Pariset, *Histoire de la fabrique lyonnaise: étude sur le régime social et economique de l'industrie de la soie à Lyon, depuis de XVIe siècle*, Lyon: A. Rey, 1901, p. 355.

[6] Thouvenin, *op. cit.*, Vol. 36, p. 37.

[7] Pariset, *Histoire, op. cit.*, p. 288.

[8] Villermé, *op. cit.*, Vol. I, p. 366 and p. 407. See also: "1848: Enquête sur les ouvriers" cited in Charles Rist, "La durée du travail dans l'industrie française de 1820 à 1870," *Revue d'economie politique*, III, 1897, p. 306. After 1848, 11-hour-day was established in Lyon, but Jules Simon in 1864 reported millers (women) and reelers (women) still worked 13-14 hours per day, p. 384.

[9] Pariset, *Industries, op. cit.*, pp. 87-89.

[10] *Ibid.*, pp. 88-91.

[11] Villermé, *op. cit.*, Vol. I, p. 346.

[12] Pariset, *Industries, op. cit.*, p. 93.

[13] Henri Sée, *La Vie économique de la France 1815-1848*, Paris: Alcan, 1927, pp. 82-83.

14 Pariset, *Industries, op. cit.*, pp. 95-97.

15 W. English, *The Textile Industry: Silk Production and Manufacture, 1750-1900*, Oxford: Clarendon Press, 1958, p. 310.

16 Villermé, *op. cit.*, Vol. I, p. 352.

17 *Ibid.*, Vol. I, p. 343.

18 Pariset, *Industries, op. cit.*, pp. 112-128.

19 Arthur L. Dunham, *The Industrial Revolution in France, 1815-1848*, New York: Exposition Press, 1955, pp. 174-175.

20 Villermé, *op. cit.*, Vol. I, p. 347. Many women prisoners were forced to perform this work in Montpellier and in Nîmes. For full description of techniques used in waste silk production see Pariset, *Industries, op. cit.*, pp. 128-133.

21 *Ibid.*, Vol. I, p. 346.

22 Thouvenin, *op. cit.*, Vol. 36, p. 37.

23 *Ibid.*

24 Monfalcon and Polinière, *Salubrité des grandes villes*, Lyon: p. 414.

25 "Enquête: de la condition des femmes," *L'Atelier*, III, December 30, 1842, p. 32.

26 Peter Berger, Brigitte Berger, and Hansfried Kellner, *The Homeless Mind: Modernization and Consciousness*, N.Y.: Random House, 1973, pp. 24-26.

27 Villermé, *op. cit.*, Vol. I, p. 356.

28 The convent-workshops of Lyon are the focus of my article, "The Church and Workers in Nineteenth Century France," *Journal of Social History*, summer 1978.

29 Emile Coornaert, *Les Compagnonnages en France du Moyenage à nos jours*, Paris: Les Editions Ouvriers, 1966, p. 65.

30 Pariset, *Industries, op. cit.*, pp. 218-219.

31 *Ibid.*, pp. 219-228 for a full description of the dyeing procedure.

32 *Ibid.*, pp. 228-229.

33 *Ibid.*, pp. 230-231.

34 *Ibid.*, pp. 232-233.

35 *Ibid.*, pp. 234-235.

36 *Ibid.*, p. 236.

37 *Ibid.*, p. 239.

38 *Ibid.*, p. 240.

39 AN BB 18 1420 (8133). Letter dated Lyon, March 21, 1844. See also: *L'Echo de la fabrique*, July 31, 1843.

[40] Pariset, *Industries, op. cit.*, pp. 240-287 for a full description of weaving techniques. See also: W. English, *op. cit.*, Vol. 3, pp. 165-167, p. 186, and Vol. 4, pp. 316-329.

[41] Ivy Pinchbeck, *Women Workers and the Industrial Revolution, 1750-1850*, London: Routledge, 1930, p. 180.

[42] Flora Tristan, *Journal of My Tour of France*, MS, pp. 84-86. See also: Monfalcon, *Code Moral des ouvriers*, Lyon: 1836.

[43] Tristan, *op. cit.*, pp. 193-194.

[44] Villermé, *op. cit.*, I, p. 346.

[45] Thouvenin, *op. cit.*, Vol. 37, p. 86. See also: Norbert Truquin, *Memoires et aventures d'un prolétaire*, Paris: 1888, p. 213.

[46] Joseph Benoit, *Confessions d'un prolétaire* (Lyon, 1871), Paris: 1968, p. 42.

[47] Berger, *op. cit.*, pp. 34-35.

[48] Archives Nationales, BB [18] 1463 5756.

[49] Archives Nationales, BB [20] 327. This is a list of 305 women arrested in Lyon from Sept. 11-Oct. 23, 1848, recorded by Jouve du Bor, Conseiller à la cour d'Alger, charged with directing the police in the Departments of the Rhône, Loire, Saône et Loire, and Ain.

[50] The chi square value is 1.89290906.

[51] Total number of married women and widows arrested is 41. Of those 41, 26 were arrested for begging.

[52] The chi square value is 0.009576159802.

[53] J.B. Monfalcon, *Histoire monumental*, Vol. 3, Lyon: 18(?), p. 573. *La Voix du Peuple*, June 27, 1848.

[54] Monfalcon, *Ibid.*, p. 325.

[55] Audiganne, *op. cit.*, p. 264.

[56] See chapter 7 below and Jean Gaumont, *Le mouvement ouvrier d'association et de cooperation à Lyon*, Lyon: 1921, p. 24; *Association fraternelle des femmes ouvrières lyonnaises pour l'exploitation de toutes les industries*, Lyon: 1848.

NOTES

Chapter III

1 *Le Papillon*, July 30, 1832. This journal was published from July 1832-July 1833 and resumed publication from July 1834-October 1834.

2 Evelyne Sullerot, "Journaux féminins et lutte ouvrière 1848-1849," in Jacques Godechot, ed., *La Presse Ouvrière 1819-1850*, Paris: Presses Universitaires, 1968, p. 98.

3 *Ibid.*, p. 99.

4 Leon Abensour, "Le Féminisme pendant le règne de Louis-Philippe, *La Révolution Française*, vol. 55, 1908, pp. 360-2.

5 *La Femme Libre*, 1832-1834. This journal's name was changed several times as follows: *La Femme Nouvelle, Femme d'Avenir, Apostolat des Femmes, Tribune des Femmes.*

6 *Le Journal des femmes*, 1832-38.

7 *La Mère de famille*, 1833-?

8 *Conseiller des Femmes* (hereinafter referred to as *Conseiller*), prospectus, and *Le Papillon*, prospectus.

9 *Conseiller*, prospectus.

10 *Ibid.*

11 *L'Echo de la fabrique*, #43, October 27, 1833. cf. Letters 163-5 diss.

12 *Le Papillon*, #139, October 30, 1833.

13 *Conseiller*, #11, 1834.

14 Sophie Ulliac Dudrezene, "Des Femmes en général et de leur véritable emancipation," *Conseiller*, #6, December 7, 1833.

15 Code Civile, 1804, art. 1124.

16 *Ibid.*, art. 223, 1428.

17 *Ibid.*, art. 213.

[18] Louise Maignaud, "De l'Avenir des femmes, *Conseiller*, #1, November 2, 1833.

[19] *Ibid.*

[20] *Ibid.*

[21] *Ibid.*

[22] Sophie Ulliac Dudrezene, "Des Femmes dans les diverses conditions de la vie," *Conseiller*, #16, February 15, 1834.

[23] *Conseiller*, #20, March 15, 1834. I have not found any records of this society. The members published a short-lived journal of their own called *L'Athenée* in 1835.

[24] M. D'Invilliers, "Emancipation," *Conseiller*, #11, Jan. 11, 1834.

[25] S.U. Dudrezene, *op. cit.*, "Des Femmes dans les diverses conditions."

[26] Louise Maignaud, *op. cit.*, "De l'Avenir des femmes."

[27] Marie, "La Pauvre Fille," *Conseiller*, #12, January 18, 1834.

[28] See also, Mary Wollstonecraft, *A Vindication of the Rights of Women*, New York: Norton, 1967. For example, p. 54: "To do everything in an orderly manner is a most important precept, which women, who generally speaking, receive only a disorderly kind of education, seldom attend to with that degree of exactness that men, who from their infancy are broken into method, observe. This negligent kind of guesswork, for what other epithet can be used to point out the random exertions of a sort of instinctive common sense, never brought to the test of reason, prevents their generalizing matters of fact--so they do today, what they did yesterday, merely because they did it yesterday."

[29] Sheila Rowbotham makes a similar observation in *Women Resistance and Revolution*, New York: Vintage, 1972, p. 43: "Ironically it is only by acquiring a bourgeois state of mind, submitting to the discipline of methodological and regular work, the exact and synchronized time-spirit, the rejection of custom, the delight in innovation, technological and intellectual, that women can cast off their traditional fetters."

[30] Elisabeth Celnart, "La Blanchisseuse riche et la pauvre brocheuse," *Conseiller*, #27-28, May 10 & 17, 1834. cf. H.T. Necessité de l'Instruction pour les femmes, *Echo de la fabrique*, #40, April 30, 1943.

[31] Eugenie Niboyet, "Des Salles d'asile en général, et de celles de Lyon en particulier," *Conseiller*, #21, March 22, 1834.

[32] Eugenie Niboyet, "Projets de creation de quatre salles d'asile et d'un athenée de femmes," *Conseiller*, #8, December 21, 1833.

[33] Louise Maignaud, *op. cit.*, "De l'Avenir des femmes."

34 Eugenie Niboyet, "Des Femmes dans les differentes parties de l'Europe," #26, May 3, 1834.

35 *Mosaique Lyonnaise*, #8, 1834.

36 E. Cabet, *La Femme*, in *Douze Lettres d'un Communiste à un Reformiste sur la Communauté*, Paris: Bureau du Populaire, October 1848, eighth edition.

37 *Ibid.*, p. 5.

38 *Ibid.*, p. 7.

39 *Ibid.*, p. 8.

40 George Lichtheim, *The Origins of Socialism*, Boston: Praeger, 1969, pp. 29-30.

41 Cabet, *op. cit.*, p. 18.

42 *Ibid.*, p. 19.

43 Flora Tristan, *Le Tour de France: journal inédit, 1843-1844*, Paris: La Tête de Feuilles, p. 86.

44 Flora Tristan, *L'Union Ouvrière*, Lyon: 1844, p. 52.

45 *Ibid.*, p. 53.

46 *Ibid.*, p. 55.

47 *Ibid.*, p. 69.

48 *Ibid.*, p. 70.

49 *Ibid.*, p. 102.

50 *Ibid.*, p. 103 and note on p. 54.

51 Jules L. Puech, *La Vie et l'oeuvre de Flora Tristan*, Paris: Rivière, 1925, p. 478.

NOTES

Chapter IV

[1] Norbert Truquin, *Memoires et aventures d'un prolétaire,* Paris: 1888, p. 236.

[2] *Ibid.,* p. 244.

[3] *Ibid.,* p. 245.

[4] *Ibid.,* p. 246.

[5] *Ibid.,* p. 247.

[6] "Lettre d'un ouvrier en soie de Lyon," 27 December 1769, reprinted in *Revue du Lyonnaise,* vol. 1, 1835, p. 108.

[7] *Ibid.*

[8] Sreten Maritch, *Histoire du mouvement social sous le second empire à Lyon,* Paris, 1930, p. 211.

ADR series V/52

Publication du règlement pour les oblations dans le diocèse de Lyon

Lyon, le 29 Fructidor, an 13.

	1st class	2nd class
Baptism	1.80 frs.	1.20 frs.
Weddings	8 frs.	4 frs.
Certificate of Marriage	4 frs.	2 frs.
Burials (over age 12)	8 frs. plus 2 frs. for each assisting priest	5 frs., plus 1.50 frs. for each assisting priest
Burials (under age 12)	3 frs., plus 75 c. for each assisting priest	5 frs., plus 1.50 frs. for each assisting priest

146

First Communion - no charge. Offering may be given.

Families known to be indigent will have free burial service.

9 AN BB[30] 379.

10 Maritch, *op. cit.*, p. 212.

11 Louis Reybaud, *Etudes sur le régime des manufactures: La Condition des ouvriers en soie,* Paris: 1859, p. 56.

12 Armand Audiganne, *Les Populations ouvriers et les industries de la France dans le mouvement social du XIX*[e] *siècle,* Paris: 1854, p. 16.

13 Maritch, *op. cit.*, p. 212.

14 AN BB[30] 379.

15 AML I [2] Police politique, feuilles periodiques.

16 AML, Association de production et de consommation, cooperation, rapport du commissaire spécial, 6 Feb. 1867.

17 Maritch, *op. cit.*, p. 213.

18 Abbé Bez, *De l'Establissement Religieux-Industriel,* Lyon: 1836, pp. 6-7.

19 *Ibid.*

20 *Ibid.*, p. 4.

21 *Ibid.*, p. 8.

22 *Ibid.*, p. 3.

23 Keith Thomas, "Work and Leisure in Pre-Industrial Society," *Past and Present,* Dec. 1964, p. 59.

24 Archives de l'archeveque de Lyon, Sacra Rituum Congregatio, Sectio Historica, n. 143, *Mariae a Sancto Ignatio* (Claudinae Thevenet), Vatican City: 1967. Letter dated 1824. See also, Reybaud, *op. cit.*, Appendix E., pp. 330-3 provides a copy of the contract signed by a girl's parents when she was apprenticed to a *providence.*

25 *Ibid.*, Reybaud.

26 Dubuisson, *op. cit.*, p. 369.

27 *Tribune Lyonnaise,* Sept. 1847.

28 AN BB[18] 1455 (4493). See also, *Censeur,* Sept. 17, 1847.

29 Archives de l'archeveque de Lyon, *Lettres du Mgr le Cardinal de Bonald,* #11, 70: Circulaire ... à messieurs les Curés de son diocèse, 11 Oct. 1847.

30 AN BB[18] 1458 (4698). Lyon police report of 20 August 1847. See also, *Democratie Pacifique,* 17 Aug. 1847.

31 AN BB[18] 1458 (4604). See also *Democratie Pacifique,* 17 Oct. and 9 Sept. 1847.

32 *Ibid.*

33 *Echo de la fabrique,* 31 July 1844.

34 AN, Petition of Master Craftsmen to Chamber of Deputies, 20 May 1847.

35 AN BB[18] 1452 (3869). Letter of 30 June 1847 from Procureur General to M. Le Garde de Sceaux.

36 Cardinal de Bonald, *op. cit.,* 11 Oct. 1847.

37 The record shows at least another 112 boys employed at St. Joseph; 50 boys with Abbé Collet; 45 at the Frères de la Doctrine Chrétienne. Abbé Bez, *La Ville des Aumones,* Lyon: 1840, pp. 268-71.

38 *Ibid.,* p. 267.

39 *Mariae à Sancto Ignatio, op. cit.,* letter 1837.

40 Francois Dutacq, *Histoire politique de Lyon pendant la révolution de 1848,* Paris: 1910, p. 108.

41 AML. I[2] 40. Troubles Politiques, 31 Aug. 1853. Letter from Sister St-Charles, Superior of the *providence* of St-Joseph at La Guillotière, demanded 8,500 frs. to replace looms burnt on 28 Feb. 1848.

42 Cardinal de Bonald, "La Réligion doit régler et sanctifier l'industrie," *Instruction Pastorale du Carème de 1853,* Lyon: 1853, pp. 22-24.

43 *Ibid.,* p. 23.

44 See also, E.P. Thompson, "Time, Work-Discipline, and Industrial Capitalism," *Past and Present,* Dec. 1967. It is also noteworthy that the ascetism of the monasteries resembled the sexual repression of Puritanism which Weber thought so important in the development of work-discipline.

45 Abbé Vachet, *Lyon et ses oeuvres,* Lyon: 1900, pp. 13-41. *Manuel des Oeuvres de Lyon,* Lyon: 1926, pp. 20-34. *Manuel des Oeuvres de Lyon,* Lyon: 1976, p. 129.

NOTES

Chapter V

[1] R.D. Anderson, *Education in France 1848-1870*, London: Oxford University Press, 1975, pp. 30, 48. This rule was in effect from 1830-1848, and reinstated in 1850.

[2] *Ibid.*, pp. 18, 32-33. Archives Municipals de Lyon, Schools, R² .

[3] Quoted in Carter Jefferson, "Worker Education in England and France, 1800-1914," *Comparative Studies in Society and History*, vol. 6, p. 349.

[4] Anderson, *op. cit.*, p. 37.

[5] *Ibid.*, p. 46.

[6] *Ibid.*, pp. 31, 80, 109.

[7] *Ibid.*, p. 117.

[8] *Ibid.*, pp. 116-117.

[9] *Ibid.*, p. 17. Separate schools for Protestants and Jews were run until 1882. There were no schools for atheists.

[10] Victor Cousin quoted by Anderson, *op. cit.*, p. 16.

[11] Baudot, *La Situation de l'enseignement primaire dans le département du Rhône*, Lyon, 1836, p. 449.

[12] *Echo de la fabrique*, #75, Oct. 15, 1844.

[13] AML R² ,Rentrée des Classes, 1835.

[14] *Ibid.*, Nov. 18, 1839.

[15] Abbé Desgorges cited in Jane Dubuisson, "Institutions de Bienfaisance: Refuge St- Joseph à Oullins," *Revue du Lyonaise*, vol. 10, P. 368.

[16] Emile Durkheim, cited in S. Elwitt, *The Making of the Third Republic*, Baton Rouge, Louisiana State University Press, 1975, p. 171.

[17] AML R² Soeurs de St. Charles, 1836.

[18] Franz Boas, "Education, Conformity, and Cultural Change," in Roberts and Akinsanyh, eds., *Educational Patterns and Cultural Configurations*, p. 37.

[19] Anderson, *op. cit.*, pp. 5, 33.

[20] AML, R[2], *Règlement pour les écoles primaires de la ville de la Croix-Rousse*, Lyon: 1838.

[21] *Ibid.*, pp. 1-10.

[22] Discussions with Professor Colin Greer on "psychology of failure" in contemporary minority schools were important to my understanding of schools for workers' children in 19th century France.

[23] Abbé Fleury, *Petit catechism historiques*, Lyon: 1816, pp. 53-55.

[24] Mme. Paul Caillard, *Petits cours de leçons morales et pratiques*, Paris, 1865, pp. 78-82.

[25] Philip Slater, *The Pursuit of Loneliness: American Culture at the Breaking Point*, Boston, 1976, p. 31.

[26] Louis Peigné, *La récitation à l'école primaire*, Paris: Gedalge, 3rd edition, 1919, first and second editions are pre-World War I, exact dates unknown.

[27] *Ibid.*, p. 7.

[28] Claire Guermante, *Mathilde et Gabrielle*, Tours, 1847, p. 261.

[29] A. Antoine de Saint- Gervais, *Le moraliste du jeune age*, Rouen, 1835, pp. 21-22.

[30] Peigné, *op. cit.*, p. 57.

[31] *Ibid.*, p. 54.

[32] *Ibid.*, p. 14.

[33] Saint- Gervais, *op. cit.*, pp. 82-100.

[34] *Ibid.*, p. 85.

[35] *Ibid.*, p. 96.

[36] Robert Colls, " 'Oh Happy English Children!': Coal, Class and Education in the North-East," *Past and Present*, 73, p. 47.

[37] Baudot, *op. cit.*, p. 443.

[38] AML, R[1], 1842.

NOTES

Chapter VI

[1] Pierre Leon, "La région lyonnaise dans l'histoire économique et sociale de la France," *Revue Historique*, CCXXXVII, 1, pp. 43-48. Lyon's population grew as follows: 120,000 in 1815; 170,000 in 1830; 323,000 in 1870; 525,000 in 1911.

[2] Louis Villermé, *Tableau de l'état physique et moral des ouvriers employés dans les manufactures de coton, de laine, et de soie,* Paris: Union Général d'Editions, 1971, p. 168.

[3] Rent in the new buildings ranged from 350 francs per year for a two-room flat on the first floor down to 100 francs per month for an attic room. Claude Levy, "La Fabrique de soie lyonnaise 1830-1848," *1848 et les révolutions du XIXe siècle*, Summer 1947, volume III, #177, p. 25. See also Villermé, *op. cit.*, vol. I, p. 388.

[4] Villermé, *op. cit.*, p. 169.

[5] Charles Pouthas, *La Population française pendant la premier moitié du XIXe siècle*, Paris: Presses Universitaires, 1956, p. 101.

[6] Joseph Benoit, *Confessions d'un prolétaire*, Paris: Editions Sociales, 1968, p. 69.

[7] Flora Tristan, *Le Tour de France: journal inedit 1843-44*, Paris: Tête de Feuilles, 1973, pp. 91-93.

[8] Villermé, *op. cit.*, p. 169.

[9] Benoit, *op. cit.*, p. 69.

[10] Tristan, *op. cit.*, p. 97. Tristan's portrait bearing the following inscription was on sale in Lyon in May 1844 for 25 centimes:

> *Mme Flora Tristan*
> *For all men and women*
> *The right to work*

The right to education.
(Union Ouvrière).

11 Villermé, *op. cit.*, p. 181.

12 Benoit, *op. cit.*, p. 166. See also, Olwen Hufton, "Women and the Family Economy in Eighteenth Century France," paper presented at the Society for French Historical Studies, March 1974. She shows that women were expected to bring capital to their marriages. One blatant example of the need for a wife's contribution to marriage is an announcement which appeared in the *Echo de la fabrique* on February 28, 1843.

> *G.B. aged about 30, about 1 meter 760 millimeters tall, blond hair, black beard, aquiline nose, brown eyes, large forehead, round chin, wants to marry a single girl or a widow with no children, age is of no importance, coming from a good family, possessing a fortune capable of insuring their happiness. Reply c/o journal.*

13 Benoit, *op. cit.*, p. 70.

14 Villermé, *op. cit.*, p. 181. According to Augier, *Le Canut* (n.d.), the weavers were "carried by vocation and by character to marriage" and family life (p. 291), cited in Mary Lynn McDougall, *After the Insurrections: The Workers' Movement in Lyon, 1834-52*, unpub. diss., 1974, p. 110. McDougall also points out (p. 123) that the extant pre-revolutionary songs are all about work, love, and the family. This is illustrated in the following song "Le Canut amoreux"

> *Fanchon, from the height of your bench*
> *Hear the voice of love,*
> *For while throwing my shuttle*
> *I think of you each day.*

The quote is from Droux, La Chanson Lyonnaise, *Histoire de la chanson à Lyon*, Lyon: Rey, 1907, p. 32.

The weavers' favorite theater featured Guignol, the home-loving puppet who represented a silk worker. See J. Vermorel, *Quelques petits theatres lyonnais des XVIII e et XIX e siècles*, Lyon, 1918.

15 Philippe Aries, "Interprétation pour une histoire des mentalités," in Helen Bergues, ed., *La Prevention des naissances dans la famille, ses origines dans le temps modernes*, Paris: Institute national d'études démographiques, 1960, p. 321. See, also, J. Dupaquier and M. Lachiver, "Sur les debuts de la contraception en France ou les deux malthusianismes," *Annales*, vol. 34, 1969.

[16] See also, Maurice Garden, *Lyon et les lyonnais au XVIII e Siècle*, Paris: 1970.

[17] Andrée Michel, "Interaction and Family Planning in the French Urban Family," *Demography*, vol. 4, 1967. Andrée Michel notes that factors of positive interaction (agreement, communication, and equality in decision-making) are more important in success in family planning than socio-economic variables.

[18] Villermé, *op. cit.*, pp. 176-177.

[19] *Ibid.*, p. 169.

[20] See also, Robert Bezucha, *The Lyons Uprising of 1834*, Cambridge: Harvard University Press, 1974.

[21] Tristan, *op. cit.*, pp. 93-94.

[22] *L'Echo d'Industrie*, March 14, 1846.

[23] Tristan, *op. cit.*, p. 92.

[24] *Ibid.*, p. 91.

[25] *Ibid.*, p. 129.

[26] *Ibid.*, p. 130.

[27] *Ibid.*

[28] *L'Echo de la fabrique*, July 31, 1843.

[29] *Ibid.*, June 15, 1844.

[30] *Ibid.*, April 30, 1844.

[31] *Ibid.*, June 30, 1844.

[32] J.B. Monfalcon, *Conseil d'hygiene et de salubrité du département du Rhône*, Lyon: Nigon, 1851, p. 513.

[33] *Tribune Lyonnaise*, December 1845.

[34] Thouvenin, "De l'Influence que l'industrie exerce sur la santé des populations dans les grands centres manufacturiers," *Annales d'hygiène publique et de medecin légale*, vol. 37, p. 89.

[35] Actes de mariages, Croix-Rousse, 1834, 1844, 1854. The first fifty marriages listed in each decade form my sample.

[36] See rules for membership in the Ferrandinier club cited in Justin Godart, "Le Compagnonnage à Lyon," *Review d'Histoire de Lyon*, II, 1903, p. 455.

[37] One out of three births in Lyon in 1848 were illegitimate according to the *Annuaire Statistique* of 1850, p. 190. Both abandoned and dead children were found regularly in the Croix-Rousse. See Archives Departementales du Rhône, M. Police générale, Rapports journaliers, 1840-49.

38 For example, the *Echo de la fabrique* on June 30, 1844, printed a story about Antoinettè B., a young women who had been fined 16 francs by the *police correctionnelle* of Paris for having knifed P. Rodde, her lover. The press pointed out that the lightness of the sentence-- which they applauded--was due to the fact that Rodde had left Antoinette pregnant four times. Rodde finally married another women and when Antoinette begged him for money to support his children, he replied by beating her. The editor continued, "Wouldn't it be possible to introduce into our laws an effective measure to counteract the unfair custom which lets the woman bear the full burden of a common fault, and lets the seducer laugh at his victim?"

39 AML, Actes de mariages, Croix-Rousse, 1844, #39.

40 Norbert Truquin, *Memoires et aventures d'un prolétaire,* Paris: 1888, pp. 237, 242, 246.

41 *Ibid.,* p. 239.

42 *Op. cit.* Actes de mariages.

43 In determining which couples were marrying with the intent of setting up workshops, I narrowed the list to all those couples who listed the profession of both bride and groom as *fabricant.* I was able to trace several of these couples in the census reports and determined that they did in fact reside in family workshops.

44 Archives Municipales de Lyon:

    1--Acte de mariage; Croix-Rousse, 1834, #36; and 1845, #285.

    2--Recensement de la Croix-Rousse, 1831-51.

    3--Naissances, La Guillotière, 1827.

45 "Avis Sanitaire," *Nouvel Echo de la Fabrique,* august 1835.

46 AN BB[18] 1452 (3825). The women were charged with sedition. They pleaded not guilty and were released.

47 Christopher Lasch, "Family and History," *New York Review of Books,* Dec. 1975.

48 Letter of Louis Vasbenter to Flora Tristan cited in Jules Puech, *Le Socialisme avant 1848: La Vie et l'oeuvre de Flora Tristan (1803-1844),* Paris: Rivière, 1925, p. 474.

NOTES

Chapter VII

1 Grignon, *Réflexions d'un ouvrier tailleur sur la misère des ouvriers en général*, Paris: 1833, pp. 1-20.

2 Jules Leroux, *Aux ouvriers typographs, de la nécéssité de fonder une association ayant pout but de rendre les ouvriers propriétaires de leurs instruments de travail*, Paris: Hernan, 1833, p. 9.

3 *Ibid.*, p. 9.

4 *Ibid.*, p. 11.

5 *Ibid.*, p. 11.

6 Efrahem, *De l'Association des ouvriers de tous les corps d'état*, Paris: Auguste Mie, 1833, pp. 1-25.

7 *Ibid.*, p. 16.

8 "Enquête sur les conditions des femmes," *L'Atelier*, III, 4, Dec. 30, 1842.

9 *L'Echo de la fabrique*, February 15, 1844, and November 30, 1844.

10 *Ibid.*, August 31, 1844.

11 *Ibid.*

12 Justin Godart, "Le Compagnonnage à Lyon," *Revue d'Histoire de Lyon*, II, 1903, p. 455.

13 Leon Abensour, *La Femme et le Féminisme avant la Révolution*, Paris: Leroux, 1923, p. 232.

14 *La Politique des Femmes*, June 24, 1848, p. 1.

15 *L'Opinion des femmes*, June 18-24, 1848.

16 Jean Bennet, *L'Admission des femmes dans les associations de prévoyance jusqu'à la fin du XIXe siècle*, Etampes: 1954. There were 61 mutual-aid societies in Lyon in the 1840's, none accepted women.

Membership in the Ferrandiniers was limited to single men. cf. Godart, *op. cit.*, p. 455.

[17] Abensour, *op. cit.*, p. 185.

[18] *Ibid.*

[19] Sreten Maritch, *Mouvement social sous le second empire à Lyon,* Paris: 1930, p. 253.

[20] Martin St. Leon, *Le Compagnonnage, son histoire, ses règlements et ses rites,* Paris: 1901, pp. 2, 11.

[21] Emile Coornaert, *Les Compagnonnages en France du Moyen Age à nos jours,* Paris: Les Editions Ouvrières, 1966, p. 67.

[22] Adolphe Boyer, *De l'Etat des ouvriers et de son amélioration par l'organisation du Travail,* Paris: Pagnerre, 1841, p. 12.

[23] Jules L. Puech, *Le Socialisme avant 1848: La Vie et L'Oeuvre de Flora Tristan,* Paris: Rivière, 1925, p. 319.

[24] Jean Briquet, *Agricol Perdiguier; Compagnon du Tour de France et representant du peuple.* Paris: Rivière, 1955, p. 4.

[25] *Ibid.*, p. 211.

[26] Gosset, *Projet tendant à régénérer le compagnonnage sur le tour de France, soumis à tous les ouvriers par Gosset père des compagnons-forgerons,* Paris: 1842, p. 79. See also, Puech, *op. cit.,* p. 321.

[27] Pierre Moreau, *Un Mot sur le compagnonnage ou le guide de l'ouvrier sur le tour de France,* Auxerre: Maillefer, 1841, p. 21.

[28] *Arrète du gouvernement du 9 frimaire,* an XII, art. I, in Leopold Malepeyer, *Code des Ouvriers ou recueil Methodique des lois et règlements concernant les ouvriers, chefs d'ateliers, contremaitres, compagnons et apprentis,* Paris: 1833, Titre III, art. 18.

[29] *Ibid.*, articles 2, 3, 4, 5.

[30] *Le Livret C'est le Servage, op. cit.*

[31] *L'Echo de la fabrique,* July 13, 1844.

[32] *Ibid.*, May 17, 1845.

[33] *La Voix du Peuple,* June 14, 1848. While the majority of the *canuts* and *canutes* met in the library, another group--The Work Committee for Women--met to establish a workshop to provide women workers with immediate jobs, housing, and food. This committee was presided over by Elisa Morellet. The committee wrote to *La Voix des Femmes,* Eugenie Niboyet's new journal, estabished in Paris on the eve of the February Revolution, seeking advice in setting up jobs and workshops for women. But, their efforts were temporarily thwarted by the lack of orders for silk fabric during March and April. By the end of April they had not succeeded in setting up a single shop.

[34] Jules Tixerant, *Le Feminisme à l'époch de 1848*, Paris: 1908, p. 59, art. 3.

[35] *La Tribune Lyonnaise*, Sept. 1848.

[36] *Ibid.*

[37] Gaumont, *op. cit.*, p. 24.

[38] *La Politique des femmes*, June 18, 1848.

[39] *Association fraternelle de femmes pour l'exploitation de toutes industries ouvrières*, Lyon: Chanoine, 1848, pp. 1-2, cf. *L'Opinion des Femmes*, Jan. 28, 1849 and minutes of meeting of Club des Femmes, April 6, 1848 in Villiers, *op. cit.*, p. 329.

[40] *Association fraternelle, op. cit.*, p. 2.

[41] *Ibid.*, p. 8.

[42] *Ibid.*, pp. 3-4.

[43] Maritch, *op. cit.*, p. 121. Cooperatives founded in 1849: Association des veloutiers unis, Brosse et Cie with 355 members; Sociétés Felix Martin et Cie with 88 members; Association fraternelle de l'industrie française, largest in Lyon.

[44] *Le Progrès*, Nov. 26, 1869.

[45] *Ibid.*, Sept. 17, 1866.

[46] Office du Travail, *Les Association Ouvrières*, p. 262.

[47] *Ibid.*, p. 263.

[48] Maritch, *op. cit.*, p. 254.

NOTES

Chapter VIII

[1] Cited in Robert Hoffman, *Revolutionary Justice: The Social and Political Theory of P.J. Proudhon,* Urbana: 1972, p. 252.

[2] Maritch believed the Internationale changed regarding women workers following 1870.

[3] Reybaud, *op. cit.,* p. 152.

[4] Villermé, *op. cit.,* p.

[5] *La Politique des femmes,* June 18-24, 1848.

[6] *Ibid.*

INDEX